scissors and spackle
a journal of the written word

Volume III
Issue 11

September 2013

✂ scissors and spackle began in 2011 with the belief that words in their purist form both cut and repair, sometimes simultaneously.

We are a flop house for words.

We are fiction without boundaries.

© 2013 All works herein are property of their respective creators
ISBN-13: 978-0615883427

© 2013 Cover Art: "rumble" by V. Smith

© 2013 Back Cover Art: "airing" by V. Smith

Acknowledgements:

I am No Electra by Katherine MacCue first published in *Stone Highway Review,* Spring 2012

At the Clothesline by Carol Hamilton first published in *Phoenix*, vol. xi, 1988

At the Fiddle Contest, 1926 by Lynn Pruett first published in *Southern Exposure*, vol. XX, no. 4, Winter 1992

ELJ Publications, LLC dba scissors and spackle,
www.scissorsandspackle.com
New York
Jenny Catlin, Editor-in-Chief
Ariana D. Den Bleyker, Editor
scissorsandspackle@gmail.com

No portion may be reproduced without the express permission of the writer(s) and/or artist(s), except for quotes and excerpts used for critical reviews and essays.

Editor's Note

Jenny Catlin always took much care to writing in this space. It is my hope that the completion of this issue and the evolution of the journal under my care that I will continue building upon the successful foundation she has laid since *scissors and spackle*'s inception in 2011.

I've always been a writer. I spent years and years writing poetry and prose and never managed to submit to a journal until April 2011. Although I cannot credit *scissors and spackle* for my first publication credit, I owe many other credits to the journal, as well as my first ever chapbook publication, *Forgetting Aesop*, which was, again, Jenny's vision.

When Jenny reached out to the world to find a successor because she had to move on to pursue her individual goals, I felt compelled to carry on her legacy. I asked if not begged to take it under my wing because I wanted to be able to give back to her dedicated readers and community what she had given to me.

Although this issue has been severely delayed over the course of the past few months and will no longer be published as frequently as it had been, it will live yearly with what I hope will carry Jenny Catlin's legacy over the years. It will live because readers and contributors like you will want to read it and submit to it. It will live because it already has a life of its own. It will live through the courage and support Jenny Catlin has given me over the last few years. My eyes, my hands, my heart are focused on carrying out her vision.

This issue is dedicated to Jenny Catlin and all of her hard work to make *scissors and spackle* what it is today. *Laundry Lines* is dedicated to Barbara Sanville whose inspiration made it possible. I hope you enjoy the pieces Jenny and I have carefully selected for both this issue and the special Laundry Lines selections. Cut out the pieces that touch you. Spackle them to your heart. Carry them with you. Read. Read. Read. Submit some more.

Ariana D. Den Bleyker, Editor

"You don't have to burn books to destroy a culture.
Just get people to stop reading them."

Ray Bradbury

scissors and spackle / Dedicated to Jenny Catlin

Tests, *Elena Saavedra Buckley*	3
Woman and Moon, *Genevieve Payne*	4
Returning to the Abortion Clinic, *ME Silverman*	5
Raised to Some Unknown Power, *R L Swihart*	6
All But Dissertation, *Allie Marini Batts*	6
A Matter of Burial, *Carol Smallwood*	7
Adipose, *Brittany Nicole Connolly*	11
New fruit, *Eileen Ni Shuilleabhain*	12
Smokejumper, *Erica Bodwell*	13
the weight, *Emily Rose Cole*	13
The Color of Skin, *Sarah Kravitz*	14
An Insurrection, *Jason Lee Miller*	15
From the Essay, *Nearest Istanbul*, *Philip Kobylarz*	23
The Art of Marionette, *Andrei Guruianu*	31
Vignette, *Andrei Guruianu*	31
Here is my mother, here is my father, and here are the people who sleep in the space between them., *Diana Rae Valenzuela*	32
Man Ray just isn't able to get over Meret Oppeheim, *Brian Hobbs*	33
Pansy, *Amanda Hart Miller*	36
Isla Vista Afternoon, *Catherine Simpson*	41
Laughing, *AJ Huffman*	41
Silent Ending, *Brenton Booth*	42
Goodbye Mountain, *Lacie Clark-Semenovich*	43
Internal, *Mirabella Mitchell*	44
Eulogy to My Grandmother, *Deonte Osayande*	44
red, *henry 7. reneau, jr.*	45
Three Poems from *Grotesques*, *E. H. Brogan*	46
The Thousandth Cut, *Jennifer Freed*	47
Small Talk, *Gabrielle Lee*	48
Stag Night, Winking Lizard, *Michael Cocchiarale*	49
The Carousel, *Linda Niehoff*	51

The Garden Girl, *Mary Lee Sauder*	52
The Gumby Interview, *Tom Luddecke*	56
For Anyone Interested, *Richard Luftig*	60
First Snow, *Richard Luftig*	61
Carrying My Pants, *April Salzano*	62
Destinations, *William Ogden Haynes*	63
Woody, *Michael J. Soloway*	64
summer stanzas, *Changming Yuan*	66
You might forget the I know too, *Dana Green*	67

Laundry Lines / Dedicated to Barbara Sanville

Our Clothesline, *AJ Huffman*	71
Jeopardy, *Lisa Fusch Krause*	71
Out to Dry, *April Salzano*	72
Lights and Darks, *Rosemary Jones*	73
Laundry Bees and the Swish of Skirts, *C. Beth Loofe*	77
Signs, *Katherine MacCue*	79
I Am No Timid Electra, *Katherine MacCue*	81
Milk, *Katherine MacCue*	82
At the Fiddle Contest, 1926, *Lynn Pruett*	84
What They Wore, *Kyle Hemmings*	86
Rural Vulture Meals, *R. Gerry Fabian*	89
Juneteenth, *Nancy Flynn*	90
Grand Canyon Mile 27: Wash Cycles, *Kara Linn Merrifield*	91
All Between the Lines, *Jan Hill*	92
Sheets for Clouds, *J.M. Cogdell*	94
Prayer Flags, *Judith Sornberger*	96
Scat, *Ryan Swofford*	97
Whiteout, *J.R. Kangas*	97
At the Clothesline, *Carol Hamilton*	98
Contributor's Notes	100

rumble   v. smith

Tests
Elena Saavedra Buckley

A silhouette of a tree branch's forearm in a small space of
lavender sky violently throws the ink of a Rorschach test
vertically upward, the fold in the paper where the lavender
touches the ground, miles away,
and the other half somewhere below him.

"A bat, or something," he said, because that's honestly what it looked like.
"Maybe a teacup, in the negative space."

"Try harder," the pages rustled.

"A day moon."

He notices day moons often, small confessional slivers or chunks.
They carry an importance, a reminder of the
cosmos beyond the blue, perhaps.
He once looked at one for too long while making a left turn
and grazed a curb, his car a canvas for a memory,
the sound of something like a panther.

After hours of folded papers, the only things that
resemble the oblivion of ink are his pupils,
dilated slightly by darkness from his self-assigned exercise of
avoiding the moon, finding a man.

One day, he found a shovel in the garage.
While koi swam in his coffee on the table inside,
he ripped up his front yard
trying to surface the other half of the tree
to find what it really was.

Woman and Moon
Genevieve Payne

Birds are going south, or else they are leaving but not coming back. When the days become warmer—suddenly cooler, when it is no longer possible to see many stars. The woman says: it's only ever that she misses the moon, that the street lights won't do. She misses the contours of the moon, it's cliffs, gray spaces, black spaces, dropping points—a hook! The woman, she says she hates the feeling of having to miss a place—a place or a name. And what about moths? The street lights murder, the bats are going hungry, toads no longer travel in twos. No one is coming back.

The woman says it is difficult, often. She is a witch from the woods and nothing tastes like it should. Her heart almost breaks for how things have been, for how things used to be and how they were. She says it is only ever that she misses the moon, she says: I become less and less sure on occasion of what to do.

Returning to the Abortion Clinic
Houston, TX 1998
ME Silverman

In a place built for waiting women,
we watch two men carry away
the ceiling-high fountain,
leaving a vast space
where that trickling once existed
in the center of the room,
full of those eager for news,
good or bad,
where the echo of pages being flipped
and the click-click of knitting needles
is now a perpetual tuning
for an absent symphony.

Silence would be better.

Sitting near the exit,
a girl whose name I forget
with bird eyes and wish bone legs
readies herself to leave.
She's afraid to take off her coat
and expose her belly's burden
but suffering from warmth.

To avoid agonizing
about the paper dress
and everything that goes with it,
I chatter about the weather, our finals
and the two it took
to take the spitting angel away,
whether they knew
what the constant, giddy-like burbling
meant to us in a room so cramped,
so carelessly created for waiting.

Raised to Some Unknown Power
RL Swihart

I wanted to make this a slice of marzipan stollen or the chocolate choo-choo behind December 12th

*

At the signal the teacher angled his arm up, wielded a blue marker, and wrote on the whiteboard:

12/12/12

12:12

"I thought the world was going to end today," said R to M

"You know nothing," she replied. "That's not until 12/21"

*

Without turning a page the narrative continues:

After giving up on Roth's impossible math I got caught up in the triangular junction of Roth, Hofmann, and Plath

The asterisk at the bottom of the page formed the third vertex, "Edge" suggested three sides, and when I googled the poem I found something akin to a centroid in her last line: *Our* blacks crackle and drag

All But Dissertation
Allie Marini Batts

sheaves of laser-printed pages,
stacked first like bricks,
then fanned out around her like
a student's ring of salt, warding off
the demons of never finishing,
a postponed thesis the first thing
she has ever not planned for
in meticulous detail.

A Matter of Burial
Carol Smallwood

Excerpt from *Lily's Odyssey*, a novel, published with permission by All Things That Matter Press; its first chapter a Short List Finalist for the Eric Hoffer Award for Best New Writing

I didn't know if by seeking another counselor, I wasn't jumping out of the proverbial frying pan into the fire. Still, perhaps one connected with a university would be different. The panic, jabbing deeper and deeper until I could hardly breath whenever I saw plants or animals I thought weren't cared for, had gotten worse.

When I entered McCally, I glanced at my car in the parking lot longingly, noting its location to the glass door that pushed me inside. There was a fly on the inside of the door so I reopened it till it flew out; the clouds looked very white and I wondered if they'd look the same if I were 30 or 300 miles away.

The receptionist didn't look at me like I had HIT ME stamped on my forehead; she had, in fact, a nice smile. She told me she'd let Dr. Bradford know I'd arrived and to have a seat. Yes, there were plants around--they seemed healthy--but I'd been less anxious if they'd been artificial. After selecting some pamphlets and a directory of White Rapids counselors, I sat as far as possible from them.

One of the pamphlets, "Common Anxiety Disorders," had red and blue stick people standing in the middle of a yellow highway with black stick cars whizzing by. On the Post-Traumatic Stress Disorder page (between phobias and panic disorders) was a soldier with a hand over one eye, the other over an ear, looking like a see-no-evil, hear-no-evil, speak-no-evil monkey. I'd recently discovered I had post-traumatic stress disorder browsing psychology books in the college library: Doctor's diagnosis of Obessional Compulsive Disorder over thirty years ago never had quite felt right—I didn't do things like wash my hands over and over again. But when I read Judith Herman's *Trauma and Recovery*, things began slipping into place like a jigsaw puzzle.

I picked up a pamphlet on anxiety disorders by a pharmaceutical company so it made me leery because I'd become hooked on Delmane prescribed by Doctor--it'd been rough kicking the sleeping pills: when I stopped, I had to stare at my throbbing head in the mirror to prove I still had form. Whenever my dish satellite lost its image in a storm--when things melted on the television screen--it brought back those long weeks when every cell in me threatened to dissolve unless it got Delmane.

I'd recently tried various selective serotonin reuptake inhibitors but the headaches and lack of ability to think wasn't worth it. The longest was Prozac but by the second week, I didn't feel steady enough to drive--or was it I just didn't want to accept my mind was only chemicals or a bunch of 0's and 1's like a computer?

I noticed a magazine I'd never seen before called, *Simple Living* with a cover less cluttered than the regular magazines. I was gazing at Tom Cruise in *People Magazine* when Dr. Bradford came and introduced himself. I was pleased he was older after all those kids on campus.

When I rose and shook hands, I saw he was shorter than Doctor or Dirk, and his voice was deeper than I thought it'd be. He wasn't what Uncle Walt would've called, "A long drink of water." His remaining rim of hair made him resemble a monk and his eyes were so blue it made his hair almost white. Once in his office, he motioned for me to have a seat and through a window saw students milling to and from classes.

When Dr. Bradford leaned over to adjust the blinds, my finger drew concentric circles on his baldhead like a target. When he sat reading the registration form I'd previously completed, he rubbed his index and middle fingers of his free hand like a pair of scissors. He wore a wedding band and I pictured a round short wife.

"I see you're retired from Parisburg Public Schools and are taking graduate classes. It's good to see someone like you return to college."

"Thanks. I wish there were more students my age though. Why more don't go back?"

"Have you heard of the Phoenix Club? It's for alternative, older students." When he opened a drawer and took out their flyer, I remembered Father Leaureaux telling me when I'd returned to Nicolet City over thirty years ago, "Don't be a Phoenix that stays in the fire too long or you won't be able to rise in the updraft."

"You're from Nicolet City?" Dr. Bradford asked. The last counselor I'd seen had stopped snoozing when I'd stopped talking with a jerk that should've given him whiplash. But I remember him saying we carried the past with us like turtles carry their shells.

"Yes."

"It's beautiful country up there." I remembered Uncle Walt telling the judge: "Child authorities say it's important to keep familiar surroundings for children. Nicolet County is God's country, away from the crime, pollution, and the fast pace of big cities where people would as soon run you over in their cars than stop. I raised Lily and her brother here in God's Country. It's so important to have children stay near close relatives who…." I'd clasped my arms around myself and had rocked back and forth, murmuring "No, no, no, no."

"I do miss the trees and the water." My eyes were pulled to the spider plants but they looked healthy. I smiled and said, "I worry about plants not being taken cared for."

"I can assure you these are well cared for." When I smiled my appreciation, Dr. Bradford loosened his tie and said, "I see you want help with Post-Traumatic Stress Disorder. How are your classes coming?

"I'm taking one in creative writing. I'm really enjoying it."

"Writing helps you express yourself so it's good you have that kind of a class." He paused and folded his arms. "Many people enjoy running but never reach the Olympics so don't be concerned about never having anything actually published. It's the doing that counts." I nodded. I was sure he was right but I wanted to write something appearing in *The New York Times Book Review* and Oprah's list. When he pushed a paper on his desk, his index and middle fingers started their scissors motion. "I hope you'll take advantage of other things here on campus."

"I go to the pool and swim. It's a very nice pool."

"I see you've had obsessions for over thirty years. It takes time to stop thought processes. But they haven't worked in the past so you must work on them being less day by day. And believe it'll work."

"I have the strongest pull to obsessions when I first awake in the morning."

"It's the time you feel most vulnerable so you need to control things." Doctor had told me it was because the id was still partially in control. "Ask yourself what it'd be like if you were happy and enjoyed life."

I nodded. I didn't know how he stood on religion so I didn't say, "But the first thing I ever memorized was the first lesson in catechism: 'Who made me? God made me. Why did God make me? To love and serve Him in this world and the next.'" Aunt Hester had given me a thick prayer book for Confirmation that'd included the lives of martyred virgins called "Living in a Vale of Tears." It was followed by prayers to avoid impure thoughts and had beautiful gilt-edged pages. Aunt Hester kept me supplied with holy cards of the Virgin Mary holding Baby Jesus or kneeling at the side of her mother, St. Anne. And cards of the Lily of the Mohawk, Catherine Tekakwitha; St. Therese, the Little Flower; St. Bernadette of Lourdes with yellow haloes.

"You must learn to take risks to grow. It's a continual process."

Yes, it sounded reasonable. The first grade nun at St. John's kept telling our class that if we talked "the floor will open up and you'll fall in the fires of Hell." The wooden classroom floor had spaces between the boards and I'd never lost the fear of having floors give way. I'd wonder how far I'd have to fall, how far it'd be before red devils with black goatees would laugh and prod me with black pitchforks. And how I'd have to remember to hold my dress down. Freud had said that Obessional Compulsive Disorder was a caricature of religion but I hadn't figured out what that meant.

Afterwards I went to the library and saw the page marker I'd left in *The Freelands*. Seeing Galsworthy's books reinforced why I'd moved to White Rapids: I wanted a place where writers like him were on shelves, where beauty wasn't another illusion.

I was almost late for my next counseling session because my fiction assignment made the time go by so fast and was very grateful because I had to forget a cat I'd seen near the library that I'd tried to catch. There was nothing I could do unless I left food around, but how would I know if it'd get it?

Sometimes I thought about being told I had only a few months to live and what I'd do, concluding that my role was pretty well played out: I'd tried to know things but I knew even less because I no longer had the oneness with the unseen I had as a child. And none of the questions I thought I'd know had been answered.

When I woke up worrying about the cat I tried to catch, the only thing I thought would help was to crumple a piece of paper and hold it as a link to Dr. Bradford. I pictured his index and middle fingers doing their scissors walk and heard his voice. It was such a compelling need to rescue that I didn't know how to ease its grip but I had to survive it like with so many other times. I'd left Nicolet City to free myself of those obsessions but they'd stuck like lint to by brother's black vestments.

In the next session, Dr. Bradford said, "The uncle who raised you and your husband were sick, distorted people. They didn't know how to behave but you're free of them now. They're both dead. Didn't you see them lowered into the ground?"

"My uncle died when the ground was frozen. When he was buried in the spring, it was my grandchild's baptism."

"And your husband?"

"He was buried on Carrefour Island. It's where his wife's from and felt I'd be intruding."

"You must bury them. Picture their funeral. They're no longer alive." I nodded, but if I saw them dead I had nothing left. Yes, I'd pictured at different times what their bodies must have been like underground, but had I actually felt they were dead?

How could I really bury them? Get a box and put their pictures in it, shovel dirt over them in the backyard? I could use a box my bank checkbooks came in because it wouldn't need much digging. Or should I use a shoebox filled with their letters and include any picture I had left of them? It wouldn't be many—I think I had a little school picture I'd saved of Cal when he was in the fourth grade before he sneered. And a church one of Uncle Walt with Aunt Hester wearing matching Christmas vests against a mural of the Three Wise Men.

My last trip to a cemetery was when I tried to find my grandmother's headstone in Nicolet City. The day I went was in late fall so all the plants and flowers would've frozen already so I wouldn't be upset by seeing any wilting. There was nobody around and the wind swirled leaves in circles as I walked around the gravestones jotting down names, birth and death dates of relatives. Many had inscriptions such as: "Mary Ruyerton. ?-1939. Beloved Wife and Mother. May she find the peace." Up and down, around and around I walked with leaves swirling like mini-whirlpools carefully avoiding any graves. Several headstone inscriptions were not readable or had crumbled away. I could be standing right over my grandmother's grave and not know it: I'd never known her.

Would burying a box stop Uncle Walt's face from leering at me? If it didn't, why not put his picture on my drive where I could run over it every time I drove in and out of the garage? I remember once seeing a flattened rabbit on the road and worrying if it were dead, so on the way back I made sure I ran over it. It felt awful when the tires went over but it ended the worry.

I heard Dr. Bradford say, "They're dead. So is it you or them who's putting you through this? You set yourself up to be controlled by outside forces and then you panic. You must move on and not let the past control you."

Yes, it was just a matter of burial.

Adipose
Brittany Nicole Connolly

Kelly was a collector of names. She analyzed people from their labels, evaluated herself by her own, *bright-headed*, which seemed to be accurate, but even she could be a bit biased. Of some of her favorites she knew two complete assholes named Seth, a whore named Delilah, and a needy ex-boyfriend, Levi, and their names fit them with perfection.

But Kelly never trusted men named Rob after knowing the guy, Robert Dire. She had no initial motive to avoid him, the name meaning something between "red-haired" and "famous," both of which made absolute sense at the time, but he had the name for a more obvious reason; one hidden in plain sight. His parents must have had a knack for naming children, as if they could sniff out a future thief before they even knew the kid while he gingerly suckled breast milk from his mother's taut left teat. Perhaps it was just bad luck, but either way, there was something subliminal there, in his namesake. Even his last name stood for something deplorable.

The first sign was when Rob took Kelly's virginity before she even knew what it meant to lose. Over the years, she studied him as he snatched up other things. He called her when he needed her, needed something from her. For a while, he pocketed the little ivory pills from his father's kitchen cabinet, circular tablets to quell the pain in papa's legs from RLS. Rob would sell half of his daily spoils to the oiled fry-cooks at Applebee's before he sniffed the rest up into his pointed nose, into his nostrils that bled from the powder. He taught Kelly how to do this, and, in a way, he stole her innocence too.

Robert was a robber. First it was little subjugations; a fuck here, a prescription bottle there. He became well-known, coveted for his defeats, as his name had suggested. But his hands became sticky. His tacky fingers caught onto most of what he touched, and he found that he couldn't put anything down. Everything he held onto became fused to his skin before sinking deep inside. He absorbed the world around him as if what he handled had never existed in the first place. It began in his feet. His socks would bore into his heels and disappear. Stealing became a subconscious act, and he walked around his house barefoot while sucking up little pieces of lint and copper coins from the ruddy carpet into his large, bulbous toes. One morning, the family cat was gone, and he worried that he had kicked it in his sleep, dooming it. The disease later spread to his hands. He was even afraid to touch himself, which had been one of his beloved pastimes, and Kelly was sure his dick missed it.

Kelly watched him grow like a microwaved marshmallow, adipose from everything he'd raided, and she thought to watch him die this way, swollen and helpless in his mother's basement. She worried about how gross it would be if he occupied so much that he'd pop like a pustule, so she left him. It wasn't her duty to change names, just to collect them.

Robert died from untreated syphilis long before he exploded like a zit, something he must have contracted from his sexual conquests. Kelly visited the cemetery where he was buried for years after he passed, traced her fingers around the engraving on his headstone and wondered whether, if his parents had better sense when they chose to name him *Rob*, he'd have turned out different.

New fruit
Eileen Ni Shuilleabhain

i

Writing calmed her.
The fire inside
had raged for days
a bone yard
of smouldering earth remained
broken horizons
incoherent aches
her state
a civil war.

ii

He climbed through
her wild solitude
through silvered dark
past each fence post
and hidden mark
the green hedgerows
planted years ago
Grandfather said
they make good low dividers.

iii

In the slow unbuttoning
he left as he came
on some north westerly blinding rain
the wind
cracked black
blew terrible here.
It fell to
smaller than a moth
and she saw then that leaves grow back.
The woods
bough bent
bore some soft ripe fruit.

Smokejumper
Erica Bodwell

This blaze is fully known
to me now.
The strike of the match, the self-ignited flames
that crown and narrow
your eyes, race
from shoulder to birdlike
shoulder, jump
the valley between us
until the sweet smell of my hair singeing jolts
me to attention.
In the face of the fast moving mass of it,
I take an acrid breath,
pull on my jump-jacket,
move toward the plane's door.
If you are able to look up
through the blinding light
and heat of it
you will see white silk overhead,
then the bottoms of my boots,
then the red chemical cloud
and my gloved hand,
offering.

the weight
Emily Rose Cole

She carries the world
between her shoulder blades,
a collection of ragged knots that cling against
bone. My fingers struggle to find purchase
in the coils.

She smells like dry leaves soaked
in whiskey.

"Baby," -- her whisper opens the darkness
like a wound -- "Why don't they treat us like
people? It's just love. What's wrong with love?"

I can't answer.

I can only dig my thumbs into the tender battleground
where her neck meets the bruises on her shoulder
and try to tease away the tension.

The Color of Skin
Sarah Kravitz

Stretched between whitewashed ribs,
remnants of a blue whale,
she eyes a hemisphere of
sky through bone beams,
black gravel imprints, red and white--blood and
absence--as the ocean licks
tepid at her thrashing feet.

Is it right, she asks, *to call a
skinless whale*

blue?

He fingers a nautilus, then her,
searching for Fibonacci in the
narrowing chambers of the shell,
seeking a golden ratio in the
alignment of hand and hollow.
    Blue is a spectrum, his
    answer a hollow bone,
               hollow body.

As he searches her, he remembers lying
cradled in the ribs of a gray whale,
his back pressed to black asphalt,
not sand. He slipped his hand
down another girl's skirt, touching pink.
Rain licked bitter droplets on her thighs,
while she asked him why names did not
endure the peeling of skin.

An Insurrection
Jason Lee Miller

Only the moon lights her steps as Emma runs along the gravel road. She is barefoot, bleeding. With enough distance she'll drop herself into a grassy spot to rub her feet and decide which direction to limp. But for now she runs, her thin flowered nightgown matted to her body by the wind and sweat she makes from a muggy Kentucky night. Emma pulls a wet strand of hair from her face, makes herself into a droplet, inserts herself into the breeze. She curses herself for becoming a stereotype: barefoot, three months pregnant, a double-wide bruise on her cheek.

The road steepens to the point Emma must drop her hands to the gravel for balance and taste the dust swirling up as she pushes her body along. Billy Carl hadn't bothered past the driveway, had kicked a kerosene can into the garden, had cursed her and gone back inside, slamming the screen door behind him. This she knows: that she can stop running, that Billy Carl had probably cracked another beer and was by now at the precipice of drunken sleep in front of the TV, but she wants to remember the stinging in her feet and her laboring for breath as she mounts Bayless Hill. As she does so, the crickets sing their mating songs. She wants to tell them not to bother.

At the top, near a stretch of hill where a person can find blackberries, the moon lights the steps of another. Against the backdrop of endless trees the figure rounds the bend in the road, one hand gripping the stitch in her side, the other balled up and pumping. Like a surprised tornado, Emma slides to a stop, immediately notices how the pain in her feet is both sharp and dull. The woman slows up as she approaches Emma, lets her free arm swing loosely at her side. A thick mess of curly brown hair, the shape of her plump body beneath a t-shirt and pink pajama pants gives her away.

Mamie Thompson lives on the other side of Bayless Hill in a single-wide, or a "half-house" as she calls it. It sits next to a century-old cinder block house that leans under the weight of the Appalachian foothills, under the weight of Appalachian time. Appalachian time pulls on everything, makes things lean and droop like Mamie Thompson is doing now. She and seven others grew up in that little cinder-block house. She cried when it wasn't safe anymore, Emma remembers, when Appalachian time had crept into every crack. Like just about everyone along this road, Emma (Gunn) Craig and Mamie (Fitzpatrick) Thompson are kin. Their great grandmothers were sisters.

The two women approach one another, stop. Emma places her hands on her knees, her straight Cherokee tresses obscuring her view of Mamie's bright white sneakers. Mamie plops down into the roadside grass, huffing and holding her side. Her fair skin, from behind her freckles, glimmers in the moonlight.

"Well ain't this funny?" Emma says. "At least *you* had time to put your shoes on."

When Emma gets home, a little after midnight, Billy Carl is asleep on the couch, asleep like a man with a clean conscience. Emma figures alcohol can scrub a conscience clean, or at least mask the smell of a dirty one. She stands over her husband, looks at the shotgun by the door, considers the knives in the kitchen, the heavy lamp already near his ruddy head. Amazing how a man can lay his hands on a woman and sleep like what's coming to him isn't ever coming, like what's coming is afraid of him, too. With her eyes she traces the veins in his muscled, darkened forearms, the forearms of a man who carries boxes of shingles up ladders. Men who climb ladders, she thinks, should be nice to those at the bottom of them.

Emma clears her throat, slams the door shut, drags a kitchen chair across the linoleum floor. He's out completely. Noticing again the stinging in her feet, she also notices the bloody footprints in the entry way, across the living room carpet. With both hands she rubs her small belly, wonders. She thinks of Mamie, she thinks of her father, and then she places her foot on her husband's chest and leaves its imprint there. She wipes the blood from her other foot across his swollen belly.

"This is *my* house, you son of a bitch," says Emma, before taking her bloody feet to the bathroom. Billy Carl, the roofer, never had a roof of his own. When they were married—the first time she was pregnant—Billy Carl moved what little junk he had into what had been her sanctuary of independence, what had been until then double-wide proof she didn't need anybody. And now look at her, out of range of her father's switch and in the path of a roofer's fist. As hot water steams up out of the tub, Emma Gunn rubs her belly and knows something has to give.

The next day, a Saturday, Emma nurses her feet in the bedroom while watching TV. Through the door, Billy Carl manages an apology, a profession of devotion to their unborn child. He says nothing of the bloody footprints on his shirt, which Emma finds later in the hamper, just after she hears Billy Carl's truck pull away. He comes back with a case of beer, a sad little bouquet.

At church on Sunday, Billy Carl clad in khakis sits next to his pretty, young wife as the white-haired preacher pounds the pulpit with a meaty fist. Pastor Williams is a squat old man with small glasses balanced on a large nose more accurately described as a bulbous, protruding proboscis that acts like the sights of a rifle—a long shaft, the cleft end of which serves as the notch where targets become sitting and sinning ducks. From the sound of his voice, no air passes through his huge nostrils at all, and the old man compensates by inserting a loud "hep!" between sentences for a quick and powerful intake of air. The result is a sermon that feels delivered by machine gun:

...that in all our days (hep!) each and everyone of us should seek to become a person of LORDLY caliber (hep!) and that in all our days in this world, all our days serving the penance of sin and death (hep!) brought about by the weakness of Eve we know that God has put his will upon us to be at once IN the world but not OF the world, amen! God has put his will upon us I say (hep!) that we should see sin, recognize it for the putrification sin casts upon our souls and step wide of it, step so wide (hep!) that one foot can no longer see the other (hep!) lest we find ourselves cast into the fire of eternal damnation where there is weeping and gnashing of teeth. Brethren, God has a plan for you, amen, God has an inheritance for you, amen, and the Devil (hep! hep!) can never tear that plan, tear your inheritance, asunder unless you let him do it (hep!). Amen? Amen. Sisters in Christ Jesus submit to your husbands and put away the ways of this world (hep!), put away what the devils of Hollywood and Harvard tell you about what it means to be a woman in this world (hep!). What they offer is emptiness. What they offer is slavery. You are free in Christ Jesus to break the chains of the world, amen. You are free to submit to your husbands as Paul has instructed (hep!). Put away the makeup, turn off your TVs. Put it all away and teach your children the ways of righteousness, amen.

Emma touches her cheek, where a layer of foundation and blush mask her bruise. She shifts her throbbing feet. From the pulpit, Pastor Williams stares all the way down his nose at her and preaches about pride and willfulness, about fornication and divorce, about how the wages of sin is death. He swings that nose toward Billy Carl, preaches about the evils of alcohol and gambling, about the body being a temple. Mamie, just down the pew fanning herself with the bulletin, gets a lecture on materialism and false churches. Her husband, a gaunt but hard man named Painter who doesn't work, is told the parable of the man who buried his talent. Each member of the small congregation gets their turn just before the altar call, when those broken enough by the preacher's words file weeping to their salvation. While the freshly scrubbed souls shake Pastor William's hand and thank him on their way out the door, Emma slinks quietly around them and into the heat of the outside world. Billy Carl's already in the truck, honking.

When Emma pulls up to Mamie's trailer, she swings in wide to avoid a three-foot stack of manure at the edge of the driveway, and parks her paid-for blue Firebird on the far side of Painter's old multicolored beater. If Mamie struggles with the desire for material things, she thinks, it's only because dumb old Painter has given her nothing but shit. Exhibit A at the end of the driveway: a pile of horse poop Painter procured for a garden he never planted. Worse, that load of shit's been sitting there since spring, hardening into shit-bricks.

Emma grabs the sacks of string beans and tomatoes from the passenger seat and heads toward the door. Even before she can mount the porch steps she hears Painter and Mamie going at it, Baby Jeannie Bell squalling above a hail of bastards and bitches. Emma dings the doorbell and everybody but Jeannie Bell quietens to hateful murmurs. Mamie answers the door smiling.

"Why, Emma Craig! So nice to see you, honey."

"Brought you some things from my garden. You busy?"

"Not at all. Come on in."

Mamie accepts the plastic bags and ushers Emma inside, where Jeannie Bell cries from a high chair in the kitchen, and Painter has disappeared into the back somewhere. The furniture is poor, having been salvaged from sidewalks, relatives' attics, or bought at the Goodwill. Mamie has hidden her sofas with decorative covers, her table tops with cloths. The place smells of cigarettes. Emma offers help stringing the beans while Mamie tends to Jeannie Bell. As Emma spreads newspaper across the table, Painter comes out stubbly and smiling from the back.

"Is that my girl Emmie?" he asks, and as reaches out to hug her Emma can smell the beer on his breath. He rubs his stubbly face into her cheek.
"It's me, you scratchy old drunk. What you been into?"

"A 24-pack. You want one?"

"I don't want none of that shit you drink, Painter Thompson. When you splurge on Budweiser, let me know."

"Gawlie-Ned, look at the mouth on this one! I ain't drunk no way."

Emma peers into the man's glazed eyes. "Yeah, whatever," she says and commences to snapping beans.

Painter adjusts the rabbit ears on his TV, pops the top off another beer, and plops down to watch a baseball game, his long legs bent up in front of him. Emma thinks they look like bleached, hairy grasshopper legs. Mamie covers her mouth and shakes her head, begins washing the tomatoes. She looks out the window above the sink, then back to Painter. "When you gonna do something about that manure? God, I feel sorry for anybody driving by. Hell, I feel sorry for myself, Painter."

But Painter isn't listening. Painter is singing "Take Me Out to the Ballgame." Poorly. And with the wrong words. *Buy me some beer and some Cracker Jacks! I don't care if they never fight back!*

'Painter! So help me, God. I'm real sorry, Emma. I knowed he'd never plant that garden. Everybody in town knowed it, too. Painter!

Painter swallows, belches. "Jesus! What?"

"My name ain't Jesus, you damned old fool. I said, when are you going to do something about the stack of shit in our front yard?"

Painter springs up from the couch, teeters on his left leg as though someone pushed him. He crushes the beer can, throws it at her. The can hits the window behind Mamie, and she backs up against the sink. "Aww, shit!" says Painter, and lopes out the front door.

"Lord have mercy," says Mamie.

A few minutes later, as Emma snaps beans and Mamie settles the baby down for a nap, Painter's singing comes wafting in from outside. Same song. Same wrong words. Mamie looks out the window. "Lord Almighty," she says, "have you ever seen anything like it?"

Emma goes to the window beside Mamie, looks out. Painter has backed his car up next to the manure pile, and he's shoveling shit into the backseat. Mamie cranks open the window, hollers out. "Painter Thompson, what in the hell are you doing?"

Painter stops shoveling, looks up at the trailer wild-eyed. "I'm doing something about it, Mamie! I'm doing something about it!"

It doesn't matter how things happen. Things just do, and most of the time things are relatively predictable by everybody except the people directly involved. Emma likes to think she can impose her will on reality, that maybe if she wills hard enough it won't rain when it's inconvenient. She imposed that same marvelous will upon herself when she left home at sixteen, still smarting from a particularly harsh beating. Eventually she willed true every name her father called her, and then set about to proving him wrong. She ran, she learned how to survive, she learned how to work, how to save money, how to please a man, and how to escape one.

What most bothers her now is that her quest for normalcy, for predictability, has come full circle, closing at a trailer a mile from where she grew up, inches from a man just like her father, and directly atop an inescapable, predictable pattern of alcoholism and abuse. She considers it an Appalachian tradition. Some men beat their wives, and some wives let them. It's a drama played out again and again with little variance and steeped in irony as the audience foresees the outcome while the players limp onward unaware their story will have no unknotting. Some men beat their wives, their wives let them, and the products of their union learn their lines by rote.

When Emma found herself running that night, she wasn't running to save herself. She could take a beating, and could give one. She was not afraid of any man, even her own brute of a man who had wrapped the electrical cord of the iron around his great fist and had missed her by inches. Emma ran to break a pattern, to keep history from repeating itself. She ran for the child inside her. When Mamie appeared from the other side of the hill, she had been running to get out of range of Painter's .45, which he had swung around the trailer, pointing intermittently at one of three Mamies before his bloodshot eyes. When Mamie appeared out of the darkness that night, Emma knew something had to be done, that these men had to be taught a lesson, and she knew Mamie might never have the will to break the cycle on her own.

Mamie was still scared and angry enough that night to sit in the grass with Emma and formulate a contract to put an end to it. Together they brainstormed their revenges, their grand statements that this was the last night they'd be chased out of their own houses. They laughed and talked of fishhooks, of rat poison, of castration. Mamie went home with a renewed sense of irrepressible womanhood. Emma went home with a hunch Mamie would never follow through.

Painter swings open the storm door, totters in front of it, his face drooping, his mouth cocked. "Mamie, baby, get me a glass of water."

Emma watches as Mamie fills a glass and walks it over to him.

"No, I don't want to drink it," says Painter. "I want you to throw it in my face."

"What?"

"I want you to throw it my face. Hurry, now! I'm goin' pass out any second."

Mamie doesn't need another invitation and thrusts the water toward his haggard old face. But before the water can reach him, Painter is in a pile on the floor, and the water splashes the storm door behind him.

Mamie steps back to dodge his feet. "Lord have mercy," she says.

Emma's chair scoots back as she springs up to see what just happened. "Have you ever seen anything like it?" She stands there looking at him, at his lanky frame slumped up against the door. Mamie takes the glass to the sink. "Lord have mercy."

If ever he looked harmless, it's now, thinks Emma. If ever there was a time to act, it's now. Emma pushes Painter forward, slides her arms under his. "Mamie! Get his feet."

"Oh, honey, just leave him there to fester. Drunk old bastard."

"No, Mamie. I'm not trying to help him. Get his feet and help me carry him to the car. We're going to teach him a lesson, maybe the last lesson of his miserable life."

Mamie hesitates, stands there frozen.

"Mamie, come on! Remember what we talked about? This shit has to end, and for you, it's going to end today. Now get his feet."

Mamie drops her hand from her mouth, drops the dish towel by the sink, and slowly walks over. Emma sees the uncertainty in her eyes. "You just gonna stand there and take it forever? First you, then Jeannie Bell, you know it. Go on, now! Get'em!"

Mamie stoops down, and the two of them lug Painter out the door. Though a thin man, Painter's weight is in his length. His rear end thumps the wooden steps. "Careful, Emma."

"Careful my ass. I hope we split him in two." Emma leads the body to the driver's side of Painter's car, drops him like a sack to the ground, his head bouncing off the back tire.

"Now what?" Mamie asks.

Emma wipes the sweat from her forehead with the back of her hand. "Now we put him the driver's seat."

"Then what?" Mamie stands with her hand on her hips, her eyes wide like light blue saucers.

Emma tells her not to worry about then-what, just to help her get Painter in the seat. Mamie complies, and then watches as Emma knocks the shit-filled car out of gear and shuts the door. Emma goes around to the front of the car, places her foot on the bumper.

Mamie gasps. "Emma! Emma, honey, stop!"

"No, this is it, Mamie. He'll never quit. If you won't save yourself, then I'll have to do it for you." Emma pushes with her foot, and the car rocks. She gives it two more hard shoves, and before Mamie can complete her protest that she'll be all alone, the car rolls backward along a crush of gravel, to the end of the sloped driveway, across the narrow road and toward the grassy embankment, the other side of which is nothing but blue Kentucky sky.

Mamie cries out, runs after the car as it gains speed across the road. But before she can reach it, Painter's old beater comes to a neat stop on the grassy embankment, the tires a few treacherous inches from the cliff. As Emma strides across the road, her will set like stones in her black eyes, Mamie collapses herself crying in front of the vehicle. "Please, Emma. Just leave us be. I promised to love him for better or for worse and I don't want this on my soul. Just leave us be, Emma. Just leave us be."

As Emma speeds out of the driveway slinging gravel, Mamie is still bawling in front of Painter's car. There is no better in either of our men, she thinks. We only got the worse.

In small places, words don't have far to travel. Unable by herself to save her husband from his predicament, Mamie went back inside the trailer and waited for Painter to wake up. She prepared herself for a beating when he did. All this she told Emma on the telephone after a long period of avoidance. Both she and Emma had stopped going to church, and neither woman had the inclination to drive over the hill to see the other. Mamie had kept Emma's secret, hadn't told a soul about what happened that day, partly out of loyalty, partly because it gave Mamie a bit of power over her frightening cousin. And Mamie had never known any type of empowerment.

Painter did not come in and exact his wrath on Mamie. Someone passing by had discovered him and called the sheriff. Soon after, everyone in town knew Painter Thompson was found passed out drunk on the side of the road in a manure-filled car, inches from death. Painter hadn't remembered a thing, didn't know how he ended up like that, or why the backseat of the car was covered in shit.

The humiliation of it and the realization he'd nearly killed himself was enough to drive Painter toward sobriety. Mamie said Painter poured out every last drop of beer and went straight to the church to talk to Pastor Williams about his salvation, about getting baptized. Mamie said Painter never had an unkind word for her now, and had started taking odd jobs. Emma was happy for her, and Mamie thanked Emma for nearly killing her husband. "It was the best thing that could have happened," she said. And though Mamie told Emma she'd be there for anything she needed, Emma knew Mamie didn't have the stomach for when Billy Carl's time came.

Three months after the incident at Mamie's house, Emma now six months pregnant feels the child push against her abdomen. She rubs the contact point, studying the contours of what feels like a baby's bottom. Hand nor belt nor switch will ever touch that bottom she thinks to herself as she begins putting away leftovers. Billy Carl sits hunched over the table stuffing his ruddy face. His glass empty, he slams it down on the table and cries, "milk!"

But Emma has decided the time for placating him is finished. She opens the refrigerator door, pulls forth the milk carton. Billy Carl, without looking behind him, holds up his cup just before Emma Gunn pours the entire carton over his head.

"What in the hell?!!!" Billy Carl shoots up, spilling his chair, the milk clamoring down his broad shoulders, filling the ridges in his forearms. When he turns to stare down his wife, Emma forces a wide smile at him, crosses her arms, the carton still carried in one of her hands.

"Hit me, Billy Carl! Go on and do it. Hit me right in the jaw, but you keep away from my belly, you hear me? Bust me a good one, Billy Carl, because it'll be the last chance you get!"

Billy stands there looking stunned and stupid, little beads of milk dripping from the end of his nose. His right shoulder drops back and sets into motion the beginning of some blunt-force trauma. But the best way to escape a bear is to confuse him by tossing a rock, and Billy Carl, very clearly uneasy about his wife's outburst, turns and makes for the bedroom. He reemerges in a fresh shirt, slams the front door on his way out. Emma lets out her breath and begins cleaning up.

It doesn't matter how things happen. Things just do. It doesn't matter why men beat their wives, some just do. They may have their reasons, but none of them matter. It doesn't matter why some women let their husbands beat them, some just do. Do we need to know how Billy Carl was beaten by his father, watched his father beat his mother, that his father watched his own father act the same way? What motivation would justify the existence of a Billy Carl, or a Billy Carl, Sr.? What rationale would support the enabling of a Mamie Fitzgerald, or a Daddy Fitzgerald who, like his own father, beat into his daughters some backward hope that monsters can change? As Emma sits on the couch she picked out personally and paid for at Parson's, she rubs her swollen belly and wonders. Soon Billy Carl will be home. He will be drunk. And soon things will change between them forever.

Billy Carl doesn't waste any time when he comes home. He bursts through the door and pulls Emma up off the couch by her hair. She doesn't resist. He agrees to stay away from her belly, agrees to crack her in the jaw, the chin, the eyes, the nose, to kick her between her shoulder blades, to toss her across the room. And while she lies there in the corner whimpering, he urinates on her. That's for the milk, he tells her.

Though normally when Billy Carl struck his wife he would throw himself down on the couch satisfied his point was made, this beating was particularly severe, and Emma, still conscious, can tell the sight of her bothered him. He sits on the couch but can't watch TV for the distraction he has created, his battered wife staring at him from the corner. Eventually, Billy Carl goes to bed.

"Mamie, girl," Emma pleads on the telephone, "can you give me a hand? Billy Carl's passed out and I need to move some things around."

It's been a week since the milk confrontation, and Emma has quietly nursed her wounds, has hidden them with sunglasses and makeup. She took some time off work, has stayed away from church. She and Billy Carl have barely spoken. He tried one night to spoon up next to her and knead her breasts. She wouldn't have it, and he didn't protest.

Today, like the other days of her vacation, Emma has holed up in the bedroom to quilt and watch soaps. Gradually, the patches from old dresses and pillowcases—whatever scraps of fabric she has saved up over the years—form a swaddling blanket. She closes up the final edges, begins putting away the equipment. Billy Carl snores on the bed, dead to the world. As she waits for Mamie, Emma runs her fingers along the long upholstery needles in her kit. She hums, rubs her belly.

Mamie's sweet voice comes singing around the corner. Emma hollers her back to the bedroom. Mamie leans against the doorjamb, asks what's up.

"You ready to help me teach Billy Carl a lesson?"

Mamie eyes Billy Carl, a vulnerable lump on the bed. "I don't know what you mean, Emma."

It doesn't matter how things happen. Things just do. When Billy Carl wakes up, he is confused by his own paralysis. He would not be a witness to the conversation preceding it, how Emma had persuaded, or more accurately: coerced, Mamie into helping her tighten the bed sheet around Billy Carl's body and sew it to the mattress. He would not hear Emma admonish Mamie to hurry and help her do it before he awoke. Billy Carl would not even know Mamie had been there, nor was he awake when, after the deed was done, Emma unscrewed a mop handle and told Mamie to beat it home. All Billy Carl would know was that when he awoke he could not move, and his wife stood above him with a mop handle in her hands.

She says nothing.

He is at a loss for words.

Emma doesn't allow Billy Carl the benefit of death. Once he's unconscious, she loses interest, drops the handle, studies the broken teeth and blood on the mattress she had purchased. She waits for the satisfaction of vengeance, but it is a high that cannot be reached. This surprises her, the lack of feeling better or safer or satisfied or filled up or glad or complete. Sadness is the only feeling, the kind that vibrates throughout a person's body upon the clear shattering of a dream. Numb would be better, but Emma has never known better anyway.

She takes a shower, puts on fresh clothing.

From the closet she pulls her suitcase, packs it between the smearing of tears.

Gravel scatters from beneath her back tires.

Just over the hill the headlights shine upon Mamie running barefoot up the hill.

From the Essay *"Nearest Istanbul"*
Philip Kobylarz

29 Septembre [1928] Samedi. Marseille– A 7 heures du soir ai pris du haschish après avoir longuement hésité.

...

j'étais effectivement allongé sur le lit avec la certitude absolue de ne pouvoir être dérangé dans cette ville de plusieurs centaines de milliers de personnes où un seul homme me connaît . . .

-Walter Benjamin
Sur le haschich et autres écrits sur la drogue

OF VIEWS AND SMOKE

    It is a city without beginning– middle– end, endless veins of circulation and cells of vibrant, chaotic life. Which doesn't mean it's not sixty percent dead. It is as dead as the Greek renegade pioneer hippies buried with their cutlery in mounds above the port. It's as dead as the Roman legions who marched and built its streets (for marching) and ate here inventing restaurants, drank here and gambled for clothes and women, who fucked here slept here shat here vomited here and cried here and maybe sent thoughts from here if not some kind of ancient postcards by taking a rock and saving it for a lover. Anyway, anyhow the memories are so vivid as to lead the mind and spirit back to its days which are now with eternity making it so in an invisible chemistry, pure alchemical chemistry of sun (first), sea, sea air, salt, clarity (becoming rarer, but yet), and the idea if not the geophysical Morse alphabetics of islands. There for you to have it, being anything from the best in life (free to not so expensive) to the worst (very expensive to free) and wrapped in the most beautiful packaging that natural selection ironically randomly (the beauty of it) provides. Okay not so much so with pastries in their Christmas boxes replete with ribbons and bows to sandwiches– chichkebabs or merguez or if you're homesick, *tournedos frites* bound like sacrificial fish in Japanese paper with a cheap imitation of it (Amurican napkin) to men in fine suits in fine Italian made cars, the suits too, the men too, to women in their Sunday best EVERYDAY and boats from kayak to galleon to yacht that are the disgusting Cadillacs of water, flowing here and there just as smooth as money. You learn things about the sea when it's deep deep blue it is cold and green it is like a bath and how we should exist surrounded by and in a thin mist of water– our life element what we mostly are anyway. Waves that break in each other's general direction and shine and shimmer like immediate stars and yet stars we can't touch, only experience in our minds not as bright points of light or super novas or all-engulfing black holes of a rudimentary evilness but the stuff we are made of and hence completely abstract portraits of ourselves and all the people (otherselves) that have existed in the world. We name them and draw pictures with them and travel under their kind guidance and study them to try to reach them even though distances of such greatness are not relative and in their not being so ARE and we travel into the slosh of space not knowing it is just this blackness that keeps the whole ball running, the big blue and green, listlessly spinning without meaning without place name without metaphors. Here and now.

Movement always of small boats, tourist barges, traffic and pedestrians sometimes local, sometimes lost in the port. Where there's water intersecting with city, water non-Venetian though smelling of it, pond, it attracts a most interesting rat life. Elegant diners engaged in assignations during three hour meals including well-oiled cigarette cases, small tips, foot play under the table and plans for an eveningtude that creates seaside windows to unfog. Bums watch and don't write anything down, if only to memory or recognition that's so cheap and easy it comes in the blink of an eye. Elle est bonne. Even the workers make it a parade with their 5 o'clock loaves of bread or pizzas recently taken from woodfire ovens in boxes in front of their work-weary chests that have filtered two too many cigarettes and cups of steaming coffee in pursuit of the yes tired and bedraggled ever-resuscitated American Dream.

Poppies are growing everywhere and as instantly they begin to wrinkle and fold themselves up into cylinders of blood, scroll droplets, far away tears of the sun. Old woman with a mole growing on her nose as another nose, but a dog's nose, lives in an abandoned World War Two bunker and even she has everything that she needs other than the always present nothing that so icily remembers itself as a reflection remembered in a mirror so made manifest in the empty seats on the bus making its rounds, dumbly through the city and at traffic lights pausing to let out a sigh of steam or is it an exhalation that boredom mother of necessity brings. The things that we know we will never know. Apparent as air it is in a foreign country (but not too far because it's impossible to get away) where everything is different therefore by definition the same but only in a new way. The observer is observed in you, too.

Hedonism in action, full swing, whenever the sun's out (mostly) and in force under its own flag: a light blue cross on a white background. It is spring and people are re-entering the world. Beaches, coastal parks, city parks, the hills and mountains, everywhere that is not downtown, although *centre ville* remains crowded. The few and many who venture to the outer regions, to non-human nature, are of a certain open places mindset (agreeable). Even if it's just on the weekend and they dress in heels and dress shoes and it's a walk out on the rocks of the jetty with some bread, cheese, wine bought for pennies.

As venturesome Greeks, we are all here in the one great colony of an empire that no longer matters. We are of every race and nation, some that once warred against another to no avail but boring odyssical stories (the lesson learned) misremembered around drunken campfires. Nobody cares anymore about the conflicts, we want to talk about the quotidian: weather, travel, absinthe, the densities of differing wines, cheese skins. Scuba divers return standing placid on calm boats and easy seas hungry to see buildings attached to these green falling cliffs.

VENDAGES

Is it not a romantic thought? To pick up and leave one day. Leave the job, the somewhat predetermined existence, perhaps the wife and kids, to go to a place like the French countryside where life will daily present itself as an impressionist painting, the food will be so delicious, the air crisp and the skies luminous, and all one must do for sustenance is simply pick grapes. Work in the fields. A modern peasant life. Working in such a picturesque, fantastical environment can't be real work anyhow.

The first week of September the inland country (but from its mountains one can sense the sea) of vinefield and looping farmland around the long green creased Luberon feels like a Sahara. There are no clouds of any importance. A haze of heat and humidity lingers. By 10 a.m. it is near 90 degrees. The sky is so clear that when taken in full view, one etched and tree enshrouded hilltop to the same and yet marginally different combination of the next, it doesn't make anything but perfect sense. Flies are buzzing in swarms about eight feet high in the air preparing for the afternoon feast of animal and human. Days are brilliant, lasting for more day than is needed, or usual, or expected. One factor often not mentioned. It is unbearably hot.

Due to the expressive and unbound nature of the southern French, especially of French women donning housedresses and plastic shoe thongs, the phrase *il fait chaud* is repeated incessantly as mantra. A continual weather report of the obvious. The heat somehow provides itself a running commentary.

Weeks before this monster of a summer day (September is synonymous with fall in a northerner's vocabulary), I had volunteered my services to a family-owned wine producing affair. A business it was yet not and probably never to be. I should have read something looming into their quizzical yet polite acceptance of my skilless raw strength and pure stupidity. I thought that such a small parcel of land needed only some love and care to produce a subtle yet better by any means than Californian, Italian, Australian, stock of wine.

Let me here stress the importance of care taking in general. Of one's hair, car, wardrobe, etcetera. What I had unknowingly stumbled into was the direst of all vinicultural situations: roughly two and one half acres of *vignes sauvages*.

The vines, in the wild state as they were (and probably will remain), had not been groomed for two growing seasons. In fact, last year's crop was left to rot on the stalk to be occasionally nibbled on by passing magpies and ravens and greedily consumed by the Beaucerons, Grognon and Elsa, when they became that thirsty.

Any grapevine is a formidable entity. It is much like a skinny octopus with thorn filled tentacles, great glowing testicular bulbs of fruit, thick meaty green leaves (and the dolmates they could make!), and a perfect biosphere for hungry flies. Grapevines grow in a dusty almost chalk-like soil. When one attempts to walk through a field of this earth, carrying two ten gallon buckets full of juice filled grapes, the feet sink into ground emitting puffs of heat dried dust and a certain wavering of the legs.

The first step of the process is to cut the wild growing extensions of reaching vines, but not too close to the grapes or the fruit of next season will be affected. Then, it's to tear their prickly severed limbs from the clump of vegetal mess, (how the calluses bloom and burst!), then cut the grapes from the stalk, throw the firm gelatinous handful into the ever present buckets that surround, then hoist those weights down the field lane into a truck bed that is well above shoulder height. Then return to those solemn rows of miniature trees that are about as tall as a human and continue the fête.

Not the heat nor the monotony that can be broken by eating a luscious grape, a slight buzz provided by its juice, the sun, the body filtering grape juice, not the lack of conversation due to an unending workload, it is the flies that make the chore hell on earth.

The invisible flesh-eating flies curse all effort. They force workers to wear pants and long sleeves and socks. Any body part that is left uncovered is appetizers for the beasts (literally, *les bêtes*). One's unprotected arms and legs begin to resemble those of a serious unskilled junkie. Swollen red bloody chunks, like mosquito bites surgically removed, quickly form into scabs. These scabs immediately begin to itch.

The workday begins at seven, stops for lunch sometime soon after noon, reluctantly resumes around two (when it shouldn't), and continues until dusk which graciously appears at around seven/ seven thirty. Lunch is godsend. Lunch is momentary freedom. Lunch is the evil mirror reflection of life outside of the fields. Cold clean water to remove skins of dust. The absence of the taste of one's spit. Yet every moment of not working is tinged with the yoke of the immediate future: the return to the vegetal battlefield.

Lunch, which by necessity, must be light, consists of sandwiches of cheese (you pick from the four hundred or so) and *jambon cru,* a salad with tomatoes and hot peppers and endive leaves, perhaps if lucky a grilled lamb chop, then yogurt in tiny packaged packages (sugar must be added for a boost), then coffee to revitalize. The French don't drink lunchtime coffee for the kick. It's merely for the taste. Fruit is optional and on a day like this is jokingly offered as a bowl of *raisins*. Mmmm, grapes.

It's back to the fields after doing whichever ritual one thinks will help facilitate the undeniable cliché of "backbreaking work". This toil is possible only by thoughts of dinner, the solitude of sleep and/or sex (if energy for the latter can be mustered), and the incredible view and its promise of escape to the barren pyramid of Mt. Ventoux.

A COURT OF WALLS

Throughout the Mediterranean the concept of a yard happily does not exist. Parks have wide and long expanses of manicured lawns, true, but the people, even the rich, have cultivated something better.

It's the small, compact nature of Europe that has logically led her to separate her frugal governed spaces by labyrinths of walls. In the nicer villas and private homes and in older, well-maintained apartment structures, enclosed courtyards provide inhabitants with the privacy of nature contained all for one's self, rooms forested with plant life, a synthesis of the man made inviting in the naturally occurring.

And isn't it so much more human to construct living places that do not conform to one another, no floor plan exactly reproduced, with loose interpretations of Italianate architectural styles? With these creations existing behind stucco walls, if not ages old stone, with the extensions of living quarters themselves opening onto the courtyards, the ground is either white gravel or as wild as a meadow.

Historic apartment buildings impress one with their bulk and matching orange tile roofs, but it is the houses that grow geometrically outward like mineral formations characterizing the biomorphic quality of the region. There are châteaux and monumental houses built to resemble them. There are ugly modern buildings that, in my opinion, Corbusier's Marseille apartment complex illustrates in multicolor. Touted as a site of some repute and notice in guidebooks, I had passed it for months on a bus route until finally I overheard some passengers pointing it out on a dreary rainy day commute. There was nothing else to inspire talk that day.

But the houses, the simple villas one hundred years old or more (and some younger) are examples of how what was created once is continually salvaged, improved, added onto- a grafting of respect and practicality. The effect is one of cubistic, mismatched birdhouses of differing shapes and levels. From the outside, these highly livable places resemble the interior of such American follies as the Winchester mansion.

Shutters are painted resplendent or are equally beautifully shedding skins of old paint. How the roof tiles seem to undulate under the sun. How glimpses gleaned from a resident's entering and opening of a gate allows a passerby to briefly feel invited to the mystery of their singular courtyard that is constantly vesseling daylight and gesturing its green limbs "welcome". Piranesi for the first time in his life entering a zoo.

More surprising and amazing is the secret that these houses, villas, and millions of apartments contain inside. There is a secret place. The altar of life. Where the human container opens up on itself: the terrace.

There is no American comparison to the terrace. It is not a deck. It is definitely not a porch. It is an open roofed enclosure, the floor made of tile, surrounded by five to six foot walls which often include plant beds, and area to grill, an omnipresent expansive table, morning fog, blankets of brightness, cotton candy sunsets, and stars overhead.

The terrace is like having one's own private picnic ground. A place to sunbathe (preferably nude). A link to the outdoors that is always a step away. The terrace is where one reads a book while warming the body on the sun-baked tiles or a place to smoke and contemplate views of distant hills, clouds, sea, or other rooftops hiding terraces. A terrace is an invitation to exercise or lounge. To reinvigorate the body or continue the night's slow progression of dreamtime.

In the premier étage apartment in which I stayed, not only was there a large terrace (the largest of all physical spaces) opening on a southwest view of the city, above it was another small terrace where pigeons once rooked. From this higher level, the entire expanse of the city not absconded by populated hillsides could be seen, the white and green banded crescent of enclosing topography, the Mediterranean sea and its weather, views into most of the blocks' courtyards and apartment windows (although I never really looked). A most secluded enclave that allows one the cosmopolitan appreciation of what it is like to be a bird in a city.

Much of daily life, except during the blustery cold rain winter months, is carried out on the terrace. Hung laundry, most meals, or warm night slumber, and the best activity of all: watching the street below.

The streets in France contain life at most hours of the day and night. The country is so vibrant, unabashed, active, alive. The streets provide a carnival of vibrancy with songs of traffic skirmishes, advice giving from and to those who hardly know each other, spontaneous bursts of remembered melodies, the name of a friend yelled after one too many pre-dinner pastises, a sometimes parade of children celebrating a day sponsored by the city: adults and kids dressed as fruit. There is only one response to all of this. Why not!

There is also usually an ever present din: jackhammers at 7:30 a.m. for street improvements or to lay the new invention of cable lines, heated discussions after strolling back from the park over a lost game of pétanque, obsessive bakery runs for the third fresh baguette of the day which involves stopping the car in the midst of rush hour traffic and the line behind that one person eagerly becoming vocal.

At anytime of the day there are women looking lovely, men hurrying and smoking and no one, no one ever looking up.

The terrace inspired my creation of a zen garden in miniature (as one should be). In one of the dormant flowerbeds, a chunk of cemented-together quarried stone, I planted vegetation native to the *collines*. Wild asparagus, strands of thyme and rosemary, tufts of moss. With sand and shells and rocks and driftwood and sea salt eroded unknowables found on the beach. With these elements, I began to compose. Added to the mix were religious medals found in a tin box under the stairs, tarnished in forgottenness– luminescent blue Virgin medallions, blood-rusted Christs on crosses. Old jewelry casing and sea shell buttons. Half buried in sand and fine beach pebbles and branches of *immortelles*, they provided landmarks, artifacts for the eye to puzzle over. Then release.

TWO SIDES OF THE SAME COIN

Tuscany or Provence. Provence or Tuscany. With Americans, it's a battle between the two. Who will win our much unneeded crown of the most beautiful, the best place to be, or the best place to want to live (if we had sufficient culture to do so). Or is it those two regions that possess what our Malibus, our Martha's Vineyards, our Monterreys, our coming close to Europe but not nearly it San Francisco can never possess. History. A psychological connection to the Old World. Africa, Asia as lost siblings.

If the question vexes, the choice is simple to make. Find all the tourist books, coffee table tomes (there are more than ever needed, yet not enough to capture the essences) and in a completely arbitrary manner, compare the elements: ridgelines in view of villas and the other way around, the flora, fauna, foliage, qualities of light, textures of landform, weave of blankets of fields and, though imponderably unfair– judge them. Play Solomon and judge.

It might be in the way photographers desire to mime the somber effects of Renaissance painters that Tuscany is portrayed in such tones. Darkly majestic. It also might be in the secret whim to be an amateur Van Gogh that Provence is nearly always portrayed in guidebook ecstasy: unreal colors in blinding sunshine. Compositions of tree hillsides village stone and fenced. Painstakingly arranged to pay homage to the schools of painting that invented these topographies.

Provençals could not, would not even consider comparing their lands to another's, and if asked to consider the Italian countryside, they would characterize it as a completely different place, a viable vacation retreat. It is strange and mundane that these two places have won so much admiration in America. Both are unyieldingly complex, remarkable in history and possessing a perfection so fine that paintings or photographs can hardly re-present.

As the dream of the American West was portrayed in movies filmed in such diverse places as southern Utah, northern Arizona, the Mojave promised Europeans a mythological sacred locus where the stories of the past, histories, could coincide in a clear desert aridity and there could be reinterpreted, redone with modern relevance, Tuscany and Provence play the obverse role in the American phenomenon.

These are regions that supply myths for moviemakers and dreamers on a smaller scale. The birth places of the eternal return. In Italy and France, these are the regions where everything is good and pure and mystical and linked to a past that America cannot ever reproduce and must regularly celebrate from the safety of great distance both physical and mental.

LA VILLE

Take the day to do absolutely nothing; there's nothing to do anyway. Pleasure outweighs work in this glorious, burnt white rock and Aleppo pined cityscape, sun bleeding orange roofs spilling in to the nothingness, mirror of the sea. Days are devised to purely experience the day: smell of fresh baguettes cooking and infinite other delicious pastries, coated in glazes of real honey, filled with almonds and almond filling. Fruits shining themselves in the constant, reliable sunlight, lounging in their wooden boxes on the sidewalk, shipped from Tunisia, Morocco, bright stickers saying so on the sides.

Walk, stroll, or ride the bus, the métro: both come every seven minutes or so, never an inconvenience to be released from the burden of a car (a concept heretical in the U.S.). Marseille's only drawback, really a real inconsistency, is that the subways do stop running at nine p.m., unless there's an OM soccer match. Waiting for the bus or métro these are some of the types to be encountered: interested in you Africans who speak a broken French much better than yours will ever be seemingly always asking others for the time, North African men or women returning your stare as you both exchange this unspoken thought (*exotique!*), a congenial Marseillais who is more than willing to offer up his views on anything under that brilliant, all-illuminating Mediterranean sun— food, the weather, the current state of politics, the very nature of the sexes, the immediate future and leaning of the world in general, and, of course, architecture, fine arts, civil engineering, and the manifold and resplendent forms of desire.

Even the ride is a most pleasant experience. Passing through Greek and Roman architecture, modern businesses, above and below hills, tunnels and city centres all that animate with well-dressed people. If luck is in the air, the bus will take a side trip down the Corniche, past the long stretch of man-made beaches (*au naturel,* the coast is a rocky, violent one), and the bus will stop just past the sculpture of David, who sometimes sports briefs or other drunkenly inspired summer wear, and the beaches full with youth gloriously unarrayed. Not in the vulgarity of thongs, not unclad as they were just on the shores, but loosely dressed and smelling of sea salt, soap, body oils, and the possibility of love.

Bus rides are opportunities to not only view in a dramatic manner the shifting, stratified cityscape, but its denizens too as all classes and ages take advantage of its services. Opportunities to fall in love with the savage landscape, to see deep into the sea, to mingle with those of many nationalities and races that defy, and care little for, definition, with the goal, the single goal, of the people, the driver, the town, which is finally to enjoy to its fullest, culminating in beach, exquisite food, wine, cosmopolitan glee, money, fun, uninhibited sex, life.

MARSEILLE NOIR

In neon and halogen light (all the streetlights are purposefully yellowed) and promises of bright tomorrow sunlight, night descends. This time is bad for women— they get harassed (think of the multitude of "Mediterranean types"). For men, it's the nocturnal quotidian without as much traffic and noise and much better views of where they aren't. Less people. Broad streets. Fresh cool air. The promise of money making's frenzied day gone by, now it's time to spend it, even if it's not there to spend. The placidity of the port still with ships just barely bouncing in tidal flux. Emptied streets, except for the make-up plastered sad whores who were once truly beautiful, streetlights beckoning one to the next, assemblage of bars and restaurants, a *glacier* still open. Europe's calmness, openness of nighttime which is definitely not rushing home to the kids of America, to crack deals gone smooth, things to do rather than sequester oneself in family and home.

Marseille's reputation makes one initially stop, pause, and think at night. Really, the crime here is local, rather than mythically international, and rarely grazes the passerby. Hold the head up straight, walk with confidence, and no one will dare to bother you. They will notice you. To be noticed is to be something. This place, thankfully, ain't America.

As a fact of matter, Marseille at night is most romantic and inspiring. At any time of the day, a pizza and two bottles of wine can be enjoyed on any of its numerous and continuous beaches, without official hassle. The laws aren't the same. There is no law against pleasure in France. Other than the proximity of yet another young couple who decide to do the same very close to your spot of infinity as they do so, decide to remove articles of clothing in an impromptu skinny-dip.

Prurient Americans always ask, do people do it there on the beaches? Hardly, as the French have an innate quality: class. Foreplay might be begun, if even rarely, for the beaches are intimate meeting grounds where one can shed one's western garbs and be oneself for a few hours of liquid oneness that can lead anywhere: to an over-priced beachside restaurant, to an apartment somewhere just west of downtown, to a drive to Cassis, a cruise to Tunisia, really anywhere.

A few immediate eating spots: L'Américano featuring fine merguez, steak-hachés, pizza, even ice cream. Chez Paul's in the anse of les Goudes: a cheap carafe's of good wine, the finest view of the city outside of the city and the best pizzas; Chez Fonfon with one of the best bouillabaisses known to the area with its wonderful central location, hidden in its own calanque; the others of other places and others even waiting to be discovered. The city is open until the wee hours.

The Art of Marionette
Andrei Guruianu

For safekeeping we took pictures of our shadows. The clouds kept ticking by above, making it difficult to focus. One of us came out without an arm, another was missing a leg. The stains on the sidewalk made for uneven eyes, black and all-knowing. How I wish I could question them, hold a knife to their skin and make them talk. What did you see when you looked through me? What am I really when I am me? I moved two feet to the left and took another picture—no lopsided eye, no tongue, no teeth—it could have been any one of us, and no one was sad because of it.

Vignette
Andrei Guruianu

Those were hungry years when anything was possible. We hitched them on our backs and carried the days around like beaded necklaces, beautiful burdens we were too young to untangle.
From a bricked-in circle fires inched upward to the edge of fingertips kneading the cold. Small fires for the young, branches and grass to burn what they didn't yet know could be burned. Logs and coal to keep a slim light going through the night.

There were pots and pans in the sink that we scrubbed getting ready for company. We scrubbed them every day—we wanted to give off an impression. Children scrubbed behind their ears with cold water and lye. Some things never change enough to be clean.

Anyone could see this was true if they looked close enough. But the eyes were used to looking down, counting our toes. Something kept our heads down, told us to count one more time for the answer, but we never did get it right.

Here is my mother, here is my father, and here are the people who sleep in the space between them.
Diana Rae Valenzuela

Here is the woman: sobbing on the steps, half-crumpled face, baggy white t-shirt, elbows tucked into her sides, gaze dim, lips curled, hair pulled into a low loop.

And she cries because she cannot find a car, she cannot find a reason. The fog-grey street splits open to welcome our ancestor's return to this thimble-shaped word and Columbus got it wrong, so wrong, we are at the bottom of an empty swimming pool, the bottom of a womb-shaped well. We are at the moment where the women looks up at me and says, *You're so pretty, why did you do that to your face?*

Here is her daughter: shaped like a girl, small like a girl, height of a girl, brother missing and there isn't a car. My father leans down like he is plucking a flower. He says, *I love you, you know that, I love you.* She does not speak but she knows (just as I know) that we have no time to patch sandpaper bridges from our bodies to the heavens and it does not matter who loves us if we are shaped like girls, small like girls, internalized like girls.

Here is the reason: My father promises his truck (maybe there is hope), and I am reminded of my own brother and how he guided me down the leathery streets of Mexico City, how my entire family stood in the plaza of my grandmother's apartment and measured ourselves oddly against that culture. We looked like serpents trying to worm our slender heads into crusts of shedded skin. My father and I sit on the woman's steps, we glance up at the hills, we course our fingers through the hair of street-lit children, and I snarl, I smile, I am a girl, I am eighteen, I say, *I don't like being pretty.*

Man Ray just isn't able to get over Meret Oppenheim
Brian Hobbs

His epitaph reads: Unconcerned, but not indifferent.

It's not like the line hasn't always been there. An obsession, perhaps since he was a child. Maybe, a fetish of sorts that grew in him, a dark placed nursed by the lack of the light of awareness. He thought: an artist takes these things, these obsessions, or fascinations and buries it like someone burying gold in a painting or sculpture, perhaps. The secret: the purloined letter out in the open and yet, very few to see. The artist hides. That is what he thinks: art is a secret hidden, the remaining material around it a clever deception. It is because to reveal it to self is too much. An essential truth. The shining example of their lusts or drives is too much. So it is to make the thing a something, to transmute, transfigure, transform. The movement has this and it is the appeal. The dream thing becomes and becomes and becomes. Nothing has to remain a thing for too long. But for the lines, the object can come into its state and still, the lines, still the lines. The truth since childhood, the way the lines pressed down on his head like a fever. He knows the lines have always been there, but his hands are workman hands of immigrant descent better for blunt work than the handling of brush, delicate swath of paint being fastidiously applied to the contours as migratory motions on the decided surface of canvas. He decides on the eye of the camera, as it grows like a child always tending to change and evolve.

The line is as simple as in the tower of Paris. The wily streets with its twists and turns are to come to a surprise with the turn of a corner, every time. The, it is reflected in every building that the streets embrace. That is why he loves the city so. He doesn't tell the other artists that it is all around and he doesn't have to look far for it. He feels a building lust in his body for it. The camera captures it as close as it can, but the hunger is to find it again and again. She knows this. They have coffee. She is not Kiki. He loves her so, this is another kind of love. The love of comrade with the streak of lust lightning their talks. Her conversation is light, witty. She has a thing with her speech, a certain dropping of hard consonants that makes the words seem delicate almost like candy from her. It contrasts with the hard, burning intellect that he sees shinning behind her eyes. Their conversation ambles, careens, strokes them both—they are simultaneously warmed by it and the wine helps it along. She touches him when she makes a point. It is either lightly on the arm or hand. The city continues around their drama. The city is alive. The bicyclers wind their way up cobblestone streets. There are walkers in each other's arms, following ambling lover's embraces that their feet only know the where. He is slightly drunk with wine or her. He decides it doesn't matter.

She poses. Like others, but she is different. She won't let him see her fully. That is how the line uncovers. Her shirt is a man's. A man's cut. The buttons on it are thick and authoritative. She has it undone carelessly. He can see the inches of her belly, see the grace of line there, and see the destiny of the line. The fullness, the broad strokes that make up the muscles of her body, shifting, is moving under taut cloth.
She knows as much, the man he is. His desire. He thinks he is capturing him. She knows he thinks she is vain or enjoys the camera's eye, the attention. She allows the distances of her skin to be seized by him, but it is in her head, she unravels the way of him beyond the blood and bone to what that lays under his affectations and suits. Coffee and wine punctuate their motions.

Leonora teases him about it. She comes up, one long drive. She comes, bleary eyed, exhausted, but still with her whimsy and caustic humor. So many women he has been attracted to, polar opposites, waging within. Their desire is to be one thing and then another like him. The artist. The transitory state between the two and then the recording of the process. She shows him her latest paintings. The baby that becomes the girl that becomes the women. The haunting rooms in which they live. He is disturbed by her work, maybe because it is something he can't be the inside of. Miro laughs with her, concedes defeat. You, Ray, try to capture her---all my lines are funny because I am funny about them. They are like dancers or the carnival, they practice and move. I am always afterward, the last ticket holder to a show already long over, the ticket wetly clutched in my hand. The last balloons I see are floating away like red memory. That shape, Miro continues, shaking his head, slowly, sadly---they are all in the women. They are all the lines, see. He makes a square with his lingers and squares Leonora's face in it. Miro drops his fingers, almost reluctant. He takes a long sip, longer than the natural rhythm of a conversation with coffee. He shrugs, finishes: She has them either in the light or in her clothes, secreted away from the world, until she or a lover's hand reveals them. He gets to share her with her. She is in his body, as much as he is in hers.

No, no, no. Dali says once, being there. He sips his coffee and places his teeth against the delicate cup's rim. It hurts Man Ray's teeth. Salvador is dramatic because there are those that watch, knowing them as the watchers they are. It is funny to watch his conversion. The meek, quiet man, so internal, his brow a furrowed thing, he seems to be calculating. Then, the crowd comes and the new matter of its arrival. Dali springs up, his knees a loud pop. He looks to be a scarecrow, clothing flung on the body's aperture, his black hair a mussed stormy thing and he swings himself around the lamppost. He picks one thread of the conversation---it is Thursday and Miro is on the shapes again. Man Ray looks glumly in his coffee and scribbles on a scrap of paper in his pocket. It is another picture he wants to make. Salvador swings around the post a few times, announces in a voice several times too large for such a frame. You fail to understand the woman, then. He curses them in a Spanish patois. How the woman is such a mystery? We are painters of faith, us men. We but paint a face of something we cannot but begin to understand! But we must have perfect faith! He strokes the lamppost like a giant phallus. The other men laugh at the spectacle.

She writes him a letter and all the letters are written in diminutive loops that are perfect in parallel with each other. No mistakes. He has a last picture to shoot for the series. That last time, he sees her; she comes in, strips naked with no ceremony, lies in the small, wooden bed and rests a book on the taught arch of her belly. She has put a pipe in her mouth, and chews it thoughtfully. Her pubic hair is a dark mass curled between the white striped lengths of her legs. He takes several pictures of her and finds himself just staring. Neither one says much in the time; she just as unevenly gathers her clothes, dresses and closes the door behind her. He wishes he had stood behind her in one of the pictures, just as nude as her. He has found she remained clothed all along. He is stripped and raw. A vast ocean of detachment follows and the same passion for line is found to be just a recording, a tracing of what he has methodically uncovered.

Months later, he is to admire her art: series of objects, the cup and saucer covered in fur. He connects it to a woman's vagina. That night, he dreams his mouth is on her warming sex, sipping her delicately, tracing her with his tongue, but his hand rests solidly underneath the cool swell of her buttocks, and it is like he is drinking wine from a woman's patent leather shoe, the raised heel of it erotically brushing his lips with momentary contact.

The next morning, he is filled with such an aching passion that his heart would burst from it. He wanders the streets like a beggar, looking for an answer, the streets only steaming with early rain and sun's touch. He stops to watch a line of clothing move in a slight wind that came after the storm. A man's shirt, bold and stiff flaps with protest on the line, contrasted against a woman's skirt which rustles with an offhand music of movement. Then, heading toward the routine of the café and his friend's orchestra of talk, it hits him.

The camera has always come between him and the world. The realization is a fever that springs to his brow like a gentle, appraising hand. The world is like the women. He sees the same line in the clothing, along the cobblestones of the street, the ridge of sun, now a returning visitor past the clouds. When he looks down, the evidence is just as simple in his arm that swings at his side and the line of his own body which just as real as hers in a memory of a room in a place in his head.

Lines everywhere and he just laughs with the pure joy of it, still swinging his arms and finding his camera an afterthought for others.

The only line on the post card she sends him later. The stamp bears her finger's impression. See, she says to him. See?

Pansy
Amanda Hart Miller

We met down at the creek behind my house the summer we were eight. Sasha snuck up on me while I was catching minnows, poked me with a stick, and told me this was her land. I lost my balance on the algae-slimed rocks and splashed into the water before scrambling up again to inform her that no, this was my land and that—pointing to the lone white Victorian on the hill—was my house. She was shorter and stockier than me, with stringy black hair and fierce eyes and a dirty tank top falling off one shoulder. "Fine," she said. "We'll share the creek. But we need to build a fort, and I'm in charge."

By dusk, we'd collected leafy branches and hung them over a fallen tree trunk. We'd drawn secret maps on the dirt, spread smashed lightning bugs like war paint against our cheeks, and swore to kill each other for the slightest disloyalty.

It was that next April when I woke to hear her crying outside my window. "Becky, you have to wake up," she said in a crazy voice, over and over. I sat up with that feeling of electricity running through my body, like I'd get when I was walking in a dream and suddenly feared I was falling. She stood in between the screen and the boxwood hedge, holding her stuffed purple dragon close to her neck.

"You have to come out," she said. "You have to come with me."

I slipped outside into the cool night air and followed the bobbing circle from Sasha's flashlight as we ran across the grassy field toward the trailer park that divided her world from mine. Our collective breaths mingled with the calls of night bugs. My sneakers dripped with dew and rubbed my skin raw.

The trailer park fascinated me. I would often hide in the field across from the bus stop when I waited for the yellow bus to return Sasha to me, and I would spy on the mothers smoking cigarettes and slinging babies onto their hips while they complained about their boyfriends. I ate it up. In my little homeschooled mind, my big house and even-keeled parents were dull, and I craved any sense of *badness*. Sasha didn't like to talk about the trailer park or about her mom who slept all day. I didn't like to talk about how my mom and dad always hugged me really hard before I went out to play, but I was quick to tell her how they would both say, "If you're going out to play with Sasha, be careful." That was our badge of honor.

Sasha stopped inside the thick patch of woods that separated the field from the trailer park, and a stray cat scampered away from us. The two rows of trailers were set parallel to each other, angled away from the gravel path in the middle. Three guys sat on lawn chairs on the path, drinking beer and laughing.

Sasha turned to me, her face blotched and puffy from crying, and whispered, "We have to be quiet. The people out at night aren't the good people." She still held that little dragon hunched up into the crook of her arm. I got this sudden urge to say something funny, something that would mean everything was normal for us again. Something like "up your nose with a rubber hose" or "where's the beef?" But I stayed silent.

I followed her around the perimeter, picking a path among the discarded trash and random shrubs, until we stopped beside her trailer. I knew which one was hers because I'd spied on her, soon after we first became friends, when she was leaving for school. Even throughout my continuous whining later that day, Sasha refused to invite me inside. When I asked a series of questions, most of them remarking on the size of the trailer and starting with "How do you even..." she finally hit me, beat into me with her fists, twisted one of my nipples so hard it hurt for days. I came to the trailer park two days later while she was in school and hoisted myself up to peer through the windows, which had dark curtains over them anyway, and I couldn't see a thing. So my sore nipple and I went away without ever seeing inside, and it became a joke between us, how she wouldn't let me in and I kept saying I would break in anyhow.

But I knew now that I was about to be invited in. Sasha put her hand on the side of the trailer, her palm flat, and held it there firmly. Her breathing slowed. She looked at me squarely and said, "Don't be an asshole like you usually are."

"Okay," I said as I followed her inside into warm, stale air that stunk of old cigarettes, beer, and urine. The benches and table were cluttered with piles of clothes, crushed beer cans, an overflowing ashtray, unopened mail, used paper plates, and a hand-mirror holding a razor blade and rolled-up paper. The claustrophobia clawed at my throat. Sasha shone the flashlight through the doorway framed on one side by the small stove, and on the other, a mirrored closet door. Through the doorway was the only bed—no floor space, just the bed jammed against the doorway—and on the double bed was a woman who looked like an adult version of Sasha.

The woman wore only blue underwear and a tee-shirt that had risen up around her body. A trail of dried blood stuck to the skin under her nose and her hair looked greasy. Sasha sat down on the side of the bed, her legs still out the doorway. She stretched the woman's tee-shirt down a little bit, laid her hand on the woman's shoulder, just like she had done to the exterior of the trailer, and said, "I shut her eyes. After it happened." She gestured to the razor blade and hand-mirror and I nodded like I understood.

Then I caught sight of myself in the mirrored closet door, standing beside her and this dead woman, and something in me broke. I bolted out the trailer door, stumbling down the crooked wooden steps and falling before I got my footing again and ran as fast as I could into the darkness of the woods, with no thought whatsoever about Sasha's attempts at quiet or the men outside who may or may not be the good people.

Sasha found me vomiting in the woods.

"Some friend," she said. She laughed, a weak imitation of her real laugh. "I guess I forgot you were such a pansy."

In the dim moonlight, I could only see her outline, not the features of her face. I wanted to hug her, but I did the only thing that felt comfortable, which was to insult her. "I'm a pansy because my mom doesn't die in the middle of the night?"

Then she punched me, over and over. I tried to fight back but barely managed to cover my face and ribs. When I let out a big sob, she stopped and put her arm around me and told me it was okay, that everything would be okay. So I put my snotty head on her shoulder and snuggled in, because I had no idea how anything could be okay again.

"What happens now?" I asked.

"When it happened to my cousin's mom, my cousin got taken away to live at a foster home. But that was a while ago, and now my other aunt, who isn't really even related to my cousin, is old enough that I could probably go live with her."

I felt my breath catch on this idea that *it* happened to a lot of people Sasha knew, and I told Sasha we should get my parents involved in this whole thing.

On the way back to my house, we walked silently and slightly apart. We let ourselves into my house, and for the first time it occurred to me that we had been gone several hours and I might have been missed. But the house remained quiet.

"Stay here," I said to Sasha as she sat on my bed. She didn't have the purple dragon anymore, one of the things lost somewhere during our journey.

The door to my parents' room was open, as always, and through their double-window, I could see the sky just starting to lighten. I stood at their bed, watching them breathe. Both of them slept in old tee-shirts and flannel shorts. They looked like they could be on a mattress commercial. This was the aspect about my parents I'd always struggled with, the very ordinariness of them, their dislike of confrontation, their good-natured patience, their habits of not lying or trying to be someone else. All of this had seemed so boring to me before that night.

My mom rolled over sleepily, only starting awake when she heard my voice.

"Sasha's mom is dead and we don't know what to do."

And there it was—the shock I needed to see. The disbelief in both their faces as they sat up in the bed.

I told them Sasha was in my bedroom, but they clung to me tightly before saying we'd talk lots later. We went downstairs to my room together, clumsy on the stairs, my mom with her arm around my shoulders and my dad a stair behind.

Dad called the police, and then got in the car to go over to the trailer park, too. Sirens screamed past our house. I'd heard sirens before, but they sounded different this time. I pictured the whole trailer park waking up and watching the scene, reminiscing about the time the exact same thing had happened to someone else they knew.

Mom sat between Sasha and me, with an arm around both of us, and she asked Sasha if she had any relatives. Sasha said the whole bit about her aunt again, and then she added, "That aunt doesn't live in Maryland. She lives in Florida."

I jumped up to face her. "You mean you'd have to live in Florida?"

She nodded. "Unless I come live with you."

Mom was still sitting beside her, with her arm around her. I noticed Mom had at some point donned a robe, probably so she wouldn't be braless around Sasha, and I thought again of Sasha's mom's blue underwear, how it had silver stitching and a hole in the threadbare cotton just under the waistband.

Mom looked at me, nodded, started to say something, then stopped and started again. "Let's take things one day at a time, okay?" She pressed her hand against Sasha's cheek, pulling Sasha's head closer and then stroking her hair, just like she did with me when I was upset.

I stood in front of them awkwardly, thinking about the annoying way Sasha seemed to fit perfectly into my mom's arms. Finally I sat back down, and Mom returned her other arm to my shoulder. The three of us sat this way in silence, like we were trying on this new idea for size, until the police came to talk to Sasha.

But it never came to that. Sasha's aunt, twenty-eight at the time, with big gold hooped earrings and those jelly shoes that Sasha hated, did come to claim her, just days later. I waited for what seemed like an interminable time down at the creek where we'd agreed to say goodbye. I stomped the ground, which hurt my foot like hell. When I heard her laughter from behind a maple tree, I grabbed her and pushed her down, rolling with her one last time. Then she rose, hugged me quickly, and walked away from me. I sneaked behind her at a distance as she walked through the field. I watched from the edge of the trailer park as her aunt, whom I immediately disliked, talked at Sasha about the Florida weather while she finished her cigarette and then got into the car. It wasn't until Sasha was about to fold herself into the car, too, that she looked at exactly where I was hiding, rolled her eyes, and pointed toward her aunt's side of the car. I laughed. Then I cried some more.

For the year or so after she moved, we wrote each other every month or two. Then her letters, never long or detailed, just stopped coming.

For all my wanderings and my need to explore, I have settled on the same street as my parents, about a mile south of them, with the same creek running through my backyard and a new McMansion between our properties, where the trailer park used to be.

It's odd that the April rains that coax the creek into believing it's a stream always seem to bring about other change, too. My divorce is finalized now. My ex has moved several states away so he can live his life without good judgment, away from my watchful eye, and I've moved here. It is only me and my four-year-old daughter, Tia, at the house.

Sasha's one of those ghost-like people that defy the internet. I am not. There are trails of me everywhere: publications, announcements of promotion and tenure, a sequence of deeds for houses I've long since sold. I have 649 friends, but Sasha isn't one of them.

So it's a surprise when the picture of us comes in the mail this afternoon in an envelope with no return address, postmarked in Texas. The Poloroid has been scanned, printed onto regular paper, and cut into a three inch square. In the picture, Sasha and I smile at my mom, who's holding the camera. We're cheek to cheek, our arms around each other and the creek in the background. We both have our hair in ponytails, we're splattered with mud, and we're squeezing each other too tightly. When I squint, I can almost see the scratches and bruises on our skinny arms and legs. The note scrawled on the back of the tiny square says, "Up your nose with a rubber hose. Love always, Sasha."

The physical memory of our child-bodies floods me with loss, but I stand staring at the picture for several minutes before I'm able to release the sobs that sit heavy in my throat. It's like her to send such a thing, without answering any of the questions I'd have for her. How has she been? What does she look like now? Did she find love? Happiness? Does she need anything? I have money, time to talk, time to listen. She could move close and we could sit on my back porch with the lovely view and reminisce. I have willow trees in my back yard, for God's sake; what could be more evocative of good conversation? I think how different my letter to her would have been, how long and filled with explanations and validations.

Tia is out back chasing the pair of rabbits that frequent our yard. I show her the picture of my best friend and me. "We used to play together. Right here in this same creek that you and I play in, that you'll play in someday with your own friends."

Tia's eyes are wide and bright as they take in the muddy girls in the picture. "You were never that young."

"I was, and someday you'll be as old as I am now."

She laughs, stares wildly at the picture some more, and tells me yet again that I'm the funniest old person she knows. "I want a friend like that."

"Me, too," I say.

Later that evening, after dinner, Tia and I lie swinging in the hammock on the back porch. The lightning bugs blink and the rain hangs heavy in the air. The fibrous white cords of the hammock are slightly damp; the grass and willow branches are a deep healthy green. Tia and I lie head to foot so we can see each other while we talk.

"I ate that paper," she tells me with a smile.

"What paper?" I ask.

"The picture of you and your friend." She wraps her arms around her belly and pats it.

"Of me and Sasha? You ate it? You mean you put it in your mouth, chewed it, and swallowed it?"

"I couldn't help it." She laughs and pats her belly again. "I loved it that much." She wears a contented smile as she looks out into the yard at the lightning bugs. Sasha would have loved Tia's simplicity, her honesty, her disdain for reasonableness.

I ask Tia, "Did you know that if you smear a lightning bug against your cheeks, it looks like war paint?"

Isla Vista Afternoon
Catherine Simpson

The air is bleak and warmcold—
Rolling off the ocean oilsalted, strange,
Wintry, fishy, sunbaked, thick—

It curls the blond hair off the thin
Shoulders of passing girls, their white lace
Shorts cutting into their ass cheeks.

It ripples the cigarette smoke of
Young men smoking on their porches,
Their eyes behind polarized aviator lens.

It lifts the small hairs at the base
Of one's spine and it mixes with the heat
Of the skin and it slides and bends

Over the bright bare limbs of passing
Strangers, it clothes them in a raiment
Of supple gold above their flipflops.

Laughing
AJ Huffman

in locked bathrooms at stiletto-wearing dogs
that think we are nuts. Crack us, we shine
like sunned tequila and moonlit kayaks.
In elevators shaped like coffins, we rise
to secret heights. In code, modeling:
silicon has hold nothing to us. Shaking
sideways, through corridors best left
forgotten. We whisper our dreams
that always seem to echo backwards. Streaming
stop-motion movies. But what's in a name?
Nothing, but spelling, spacing and semantics.
Relax. Lean back and let the popped-
corn characters dance. Right!?! Up
until dawn.

Silent Ending
Brenton Booth

Words like powerful waterfalls
flooding the silence and forming
into determined streams,
reflecting
the sun,
moon,
stars,
and towering
families of humourless trees;
with insects,
reptiles,
animals,
and Neanderthals
all feeding from those mighty
undisturbed currents,
that through time and unfaltering
output
become great oceans,
tidal waves,
tsunamis,
and the conquerors of modern lands:
words that cut like masterfully built
katana swords,
sting the eyes to tears,
pierce the mind to grow,
open the heart to love,
wound the spirit to hate;
words flying,
words screaming,
words hurdling gracefully through time;
words infecting thoughts like radio waves,
words capable of invoking change,
words diving into the great void of nothing
and bringing life to it again—
words doing everything but leaving my lips now:
begging her to stay.

Goodbye Mountain
Lacie Clark-Semenovich

When his mother died, he gave his favorite stuffed bear to his three-year-old cousin. His childhood ghost, like those of his woodsman grandfathers, tramped brittle leaves, climbed fallen trees deep into the mountain.

Clay filled the crevices of his boots, sucked at his soles as though the earth was reclaiming its flesh. Blessed by the breath of the mountain's kiss. Mushrooms grew in his pockets. Dimpled, brown things he harvested for soup.

Briar branded, wind damaged. Men don't play with stuffed bears. Coal tattooed his fingers and forehead. Lungs sponged night from the air. Fingers scraped with lava, hardened the calluses and steel of his hands.

When his father died, he loaded his saddle bags with t-shirts, stained jeans, and his mother's photo album. His gloves and hammer handles burned in the oil drum out back. Smoke signal. Funeral pyre. Carbon-drunk, the trees wept into the wind.

Internal
Mirabella Mitchell

After a long stumble through the sudden
dust, the shells of small, dead things,
the days that could easily clutter into a life,
do you mind a little flight, a mess
someone else will have to clean? It's not
permanent—just confused, a nervous
chaos, the little beats between beats. I open
all the doors, even the cupboards. Your
disapproval etched in my mirror. I wish
for more window, less wall. I return
from the world and find the floor covered
with flies, all their wings extended.

Eulogy to My Grandmother
Deonte Osayande

and it begins with the sinking
of the unsinkable. You and the Titanic
were born around the same time,
yet it has only seen the underworld.
Haven't you as well?

When you left you saw
the first great war and renaissance,
depression of drought and despair,
and the creation of clouds of men,
the napalm and marches, hoses
and assassinations, addictions
and dances, calamities of humanity.

You had seen the sky fall and all
of this and much more, you had seen
it all while black. While black as well, well
the view, of a light above this is what you
had seen within the depths of you,
unsinkable.

red
henry 7. reneau, jr.

for sabrina macias, on lock-down

a caution shade of combustion all appetite:
Revlon red lipstick that mimics arousal &
pornographic, vermilion fingernails
accentuate a splayed erotic;

red hair kissed by flaming fire,
a sensual awakening, Ann-Margret's purr,
a perfect flint to start a quarrel, or bullet
that portends a war;

fist-tight crimson resurrected & flung
into scorching solar wind,
white phosphorous phoenix, all molten red
& gold immolation.

& frightened russet sparrows
running red-light scared
& brushfire sweep of abandon-ship crows
launch into arsonist auburn sky,

before an obsession with the pyre, terror-blind
terrific as all Creation.   ascending angel ablaze
& dancing as Divine, a red rebellious heart
burning, rising from the stake, to cardinal
conflagration,

to red-shift reincarnation
at the igneous end of panic, scarlet obsession
to vaporization,
to crematoria bone-gray ash, reborn
an unrequited, yet intimate, act of passion.

Three Poems from *Grotesques*
E.H. Brogan

Expansion

Lately I've been c-co-convinced
I'm choking. My breathing's even but
food-grains linger on my tonsils,
on my tongue. My mind busies and compiles
images of my nearby death: face turning
blue, the sick topple and attendant thud.
The cats'll start to chew my cheeks
or nose within a day. Can't afford
to be too patient when you're hungry,
after all.

I chew my food into a soup, as many
grinds as I can bear, to find that I
still count my breaths, still measure
my inhales against my ex. Perhaps
I could attempt a different tack. I needn't
eat so much, at that.

Fantasia

My eye began unwinding on
the journey home. Not quite right but stuck
behind the wheel, only driver
to the screw, I felt pain lurk in
my forehead and the sure assurance that
my eye was bursting. White strands,
like ectoplasm, started to unlace from my
nasolacrimal duct and the corner
of my eye. Like waxed or wired button thread,
an explosion of eyewhite spun from my socket
while I tried to hold the wheel and drive.
It was a great fear realized.

Cage Maintenance

I hate living like
I'm dying. I get all
these twitches, hits of my
mortality in whiskey shots at sticky
bars inebriating confidence.
My soul's total lack
of control over its
own house's confounding
while the clockwork
turn-by-turn, grinds down.
Each gear-click is a hitch to
elicit my hysterics. I'm convinced
each turn is barely made, that every
effort went into that last snap
of place. I have appendicitis.
Salmonella. Nerve damage,
too. Body-having's such a shocking
thing to do.

The Thousandth Cut
Jennifer Freed

She has just stepped dripping
from the shower
when he stops in the open doorway
of their room.
She sees him see her,
sees
that his face does not soften,
does not warm,
does not change at all
at the sight of her
standing naked
by their
bureau.
He simply turns without a word
and walks back down the hall.

Small Talk
Gabrielle Lee

I don't want to talk about how I am. This is because I don't know if I am okay, and I don't like to be dishonest. You expect me to fall into the synced-up rhythms of *how-are-you-I'm-fine*, but I refuse. It's not because I'm a hippie, or because I have some vendetta against lying, or liars, or have some extensive Christian moral code, or that I care if you think I'm neurotic or even that I want to share my life story with you. I don't want to talk about it because I don't want to think about it, because when I think about it I have panic attacks and I don't like having panic attacks. They make me panicked. I don't like being panicked. It makes my heart race and I start to contemplate the meaning of my life and whether I'm a good enough person and if I've been working out enough lately and whether my mom likes me and if I've been serving my community in an adequate fashion and how I narrowly missed my flight this morning because it was at six A.M. and I almost didn't get up and whether the plane will go down or not and whether I should resort to cannibalism if the plane crashes and we're all stranded on a desert island just like people ask you in hypothetical questions that are really not-so-hypothetical after all because the plane will probably crash and I will probably die in it because most people are rather shoddy under pressure but I'm not but I don't like the responsibility of sitting in the emergency exit row. A lot of people like the leg room but I would rather curl up in a ball in a window seat, lean my head against the cabin's plastic siding, and try not to think about the homework that I'm avoiding on this flight, try not to think about how miserable I'll be away from my husband for five days but also how much more miserable I'll be when I return, not because of my husband but because of the dull, grey skies that await me back "home," this once-foreign place we call "home" now, if only because we're so uprooted that the only place that "home" could be is wherever we have a space together, only everything outside that five-hundred-square-foot space feels inadequate, or horrifying, or nothing even remotely close to the sunny, warm, inviting, if a little corporate, city we used to call home, that place where I had finally, after *years* of searching and fighting and searching and fighting and fighting and fighting and *fighting* – decided I liked who I was. That was the place where I'd met my husband and we'd found our little nook of stability and happiness and beaches and farmer's markets and sunshine and then I had to go and decide I wanted a *career* and we moved and in five days I have to go back to that place where we moved, with the grey skies and the cracked streets and the winter that lags on from October to March. I have him, but we're lonely there. It's him and it's me and we're "home" and we're alone. I'm alone, even as I sit next to you on this flight, even in this community of bodies collectively suffering geographical limbo.

The smile is what you expect – the nod and the customary brief response and the *click* of the seatbelt as I accept my place. And because I am tired, because I don't want to think about it, because I don't want to have a panic attack on this plane because then the flight attendant will in turn ask if I'm okay and I won't know what to tell her, either, I'll say it.

I'm fine. How are you?

Stag Night, Winking Lizard
Michael Cocchiarale

"Ok, check this out: I was gay once. Funny story. Sophomore year, the first night at the retreat house in Painesville. Bunch of us Jesuit boys—'men for others,' wink, wink—thrown together in this long room of bunks, and Swervos or something—you remember him?"

Zervos. John Paul Zervos. Smile like a smack backed screen, a sparkler sizzling in the sidewalk.

"Right in front of my bunk, he stripped to his skivvies, and, if you can believe it, the first thing I thought was *rump*. Yeah, yeah, you heard me right. *Rump*. As in rump roast. As in a chunk of sizzling meat to sink your teeth into. I was sick with it—don't need to tell me. To make matters worse, he turned, and my eyes shot up that swimmer skin toward the great white bulge. I reeled, I rallied. 'Faggot, put some sweatpants on!' I said, which almost broke the spell with laughs."

Your mouth's a walk-in closet. In front of you, the bartender flashes quick, indifferent hands. Behind, vaguely familiar alumni cheer a shortstop sliding a foot across second for the final out.

"Then Warren popped his head in, pissed a 'lights out, fellas!' all over the place. Farts and giggles for awhile until it was just poor little me and a lot of pitch fucking black. Total silence like you can't believe. Man, it was, I don't know, one of those—what do you call 'em?—dark nights of the soul. Felt like I was nowhere, a nobody and a nothing.

You finally sip the drink he bought you, the happy hour special.

I rushed my hands to my side, and just like that, there I was again: fingers on legs, thank the Lord! Problem was, in the dark, I get to feeling skin is skin. I trace, I circle around, run fingers from knee to thigh. I see those goddamn legs again. Feel them, the muscles, the hairless curves. Long story short: The thing moves. It leaps. It grows. As they say in the monster movies, 'It's alive!'"

A memory of Zervos at lunch, sitting in the far corner of the senior lounge, that screen door swung open to his friends— the treasurer of student council, the editor of literary magazine. He always seemed to face you. You never sought his eye.

"I pressed the pillow into my face, began to understand why that king, the ancient one—the mother fucker—gouged his goddamn eyes!"

Oedipus, the too curious king. May you never know who you are.

"I'm thinking, okay now, relax. Just take a deep breath. Who's the patron saint of straightedness? Got to be damn near everyone of them. Right? Augustine, Becket, Francis, Aquinas—I fired each one a prayer."

Flicking the pineapple wedge from the rim, he kills the drink—his third—in one greedy gulp.

"When that didn't work, I thought about awful things: breast cancer for mom, car in a ditch for dad. No luck. All I could see was a full moon of BVDs, and I'm smack dab under it, on my knees now, ripping buttons off my shirt. Nails shoot out of my fingers. Beast hair swirls around my mouth. At this point, kid you fucking not: I could have gone either way!"

You nod, the talent that got you through the days your class relives now in this raucous Lakewood bar.

"Out of nowhere, someone snorted, and I remembered Lynch on the shitter the week before, grunting like the hog he's always been. I was shaking off when Barelli tiptoed to the stall and grunt-whispered through the door: 'This… too… shall… pass!'

Bam! Just like that, I'm cured. Like Paul zapped off the horse, Ignatius after that screaming canon ball to the crotch. Like the Holy Spirit swooping down with one of those tongues of fire. Para—no, no, *Meta*noia. Isn't that the word I'm looking for?"

Agape—that's the Greek that's stunned your heart for all these years.

"Anyway, from there (thank God!), it's been one uninterrupted run of tits and holes just where they're supposed to be. Believe I'm married thirteen years? Megan, the old lady, she's a regular semiautomatic, spraying em left and right."

In his strained and sweaty face, the satisfying recoil of a rifle. In your head, a bursting open—the flight of a ghost you couldn't dare know how to pursue.

"Well, well, there's my shocking confession for the night! Now what's say we grab ourselves some beer? Love the vodka in these, but as you now know well—I don't do fruits, ha, ha. Already had my fifteen minutes of flame!"

The Carousel
Linda Niehoff

She liked the thrill of spinning around on the carousel, faster than she'd ever gone before. She liked the blaring organ and even the electric bulbs that her mother said were vulgar. She liked the children's screams, the whirl in her stomach, her skirt flapping behind her, and her hat flying off. And when the young man working picked it up, she liked the thrill of his arm looped though hers as later they walked the length of the beach, the glow of the carousel doused behind them.

"Promise me you'll come back," he said.

"I promise," she said under the stars inside the fog next to the crashing sea.

Nightly she rode. Her favorite was the horse whose body swirled into a mermaid's tail. Riding, she was half horse half mermaid galloping and swimming all at once. For a splintered moment, she was free.

Nightly the man said, "Promise me."

Nightly she agreed.

Her parents did not approve.

"He ought to be a banker, he ought to practice medicine, he ought not to run a carousel by the sea." Her father stood in the study, a glass of bourbon in his right hand. Ice clinked, waves crashed beyond cluttered bookshelves. "You cannot ride anymore; I forbid it."

The carousel was a glowing blob in the window's wavy glass. Didn't they understand the tinny organ, the silent beasts, the spinning sea beside her? She yearned to move, even if it was only in circles.

"Promise me you'll come back." She held onto those words as she crept past the study, past her father, thick with drink, face down over his ledgers.

She was barefoot and only wore a nightgown as she walked across the still-warm sand. The carousel was empty as she knew it would be; the man was gone. The wooden menagerie creaked and moaned in the wind, their faces frozen in eternal snarls. She lifted a hand and ran it over their splintering paint.

She would come back but not for him.

She walked past the dark sign that in daylight would have read, "Dangerous undertow" and at the water's edge, peeled off her moon-colored nightgown.

She would haunt the carousel like the moaning wind. She would pull the hats off girls and steal inside their screams. But first, one final thrill. One final ride of galloping freedom inside the swallowing sea.

The Garden Girl
Mary Lee Sauder

The woman stumbles onto the moldy patio, her bare foot brushing against a rusted twist of wire. With a sigh, she closes the tattered screen door behind her. Nothing back there but what keeps her standing each day. Cold, bitter coffee and stale granola in a dirty china bowl. A sunken mattress with the consistency of day-old oatmeal. A picture frame covered in a thick layer of dust. She traps it all behind the ineffectual defenses of the screen door and turns to face the garden. Immaculate orchids of every shape and color twine around thin wooden sapling stalks. Rows of pansies intermingle with rose bushes and a thousand sprigs of mint.

Succulent tomatoes, blood red and dripping with the remnants of morning dew, dangle lazily over a carpet of oregano. Hanging branches of a tall willow form a curtain; beyond it, either a mess of honeydew vines or a portal to another world. The woman bends down to pick up a trowel and some pruning shears lying in the dirt. She hitches up her faded blue nightgown and begins to work.

Amy's place.

She'll be here.

She'll come back right through those branches and see me.

See me like this.

She can't - why did you let this.

Shut up.

Just shut up and The woman snips wilted tendrils from the deepest red orchids. Through the translucent petals she sees dark brown hair yanked into a stump of a ponytail, the ends sticking straight out like a rough straw broom. Kelly green overalls. Velcro sandals from Disneyland. Not the light up kind. The woman accidentally clips a healthy petal right through the middle. A gash. The orchid holds its shape, not weeping over its injury. The petal will fall off on its own if the woman doesn't finish the job. It is unhealthy now. It broke the natural symmetry of the flower. The woman leaves it there.

Stay, Amy.

Stay here with me and play in the garden.

Like you did before

stay before something

Be careful

But then

The woman stands on her teetering legs and looks around the garden. Beautiful green foliage creeping upward to touch the sky. To swallow the sun. The willow branches hide honeydew and the world. She rubs the dark circles under her eyes and sinks her toes into the rich dirt. A twig catches her ankle and scratches her taut gray skin. She slumps to the ground and stares at the willow, small tears tracing crevices in her face. Nothing stirs inside of her. Her mind is a haze of kelly green static.

Today, she is swathed in a torn grey lace nightgown. The kind the woman's own mother used to wear when she made hashbrowns at the old stove that clicked and sputtered on the third burner. Such a good, kind soul. Saintly, as she knew her. The woman could never fill those shoes. Maybe this is her mother's nightgown. She doesn't know. She had slept in the garden the night before. It had seemed too much trouble to go back to the house. There are no benches in the garden and no gazebos or marble ledges. She had slept in the dirt. That day, she had been harvesting strawberries. She had left them in a thatched basket, only the good ones. She had left them by the willow. Today, they are still there. The woman has a goal today. She will harvest the honeydews. There will be frost soon. She must do this.

Amy, I

You must

Come back

Amy I have to

I have to do this Amy

I can't stay

But you have to

YOU HURT HER

She tears her gaze away from the willow and the honeydews.

IT'S YOUR FAULT

She flees to the other side of the garden and busies herself with the tomatoes, mechanically pulling weeds from the cages and tossing them out of her sight. Dandelion scraps fly from her cracked and bitten fingernails and land on her nightgown, staining the soft gray cotton that wasn't meant for her.

No one has seen the woman in years. Not since pneumonia took her little girl. The neighbors remember the little girl, though they can't seem to recall her name. She could always be seen flitting around in the tidy garden that the woman kept, playing all day and digging her tiny plastic spade in the ground. They would pass by and notice an orchid in the girl's hair and a sprig of sage in her pale hand. The garden was where she belonged and where she prospered.

What happened to them? Is that woman still there? The garden grew around her and encased her. This shrinks property values. The shabby old willow forms a shroud over the place, but through a few branches glimpses of golden honeydews can be seen. The neighbors hedge bets on whether the woman will be seen again. The last time anyone saw her was when the ambulance came by. She was lying in the flower beds, clutching a tiny, lifeless hand and crying soundlessly. Maybe she is already long gone.

It was seasonal

Things like this happen

It wasn't

your fault it was

The weather or the

doctors

You could sue

But if she comes back I want to be

there

Leave now

When she comes it has to be

perfect and just the same

Just the same

Get out

And into my arms Amy will

The woman rises from her mattress and brushes the coarse blankets from her emaciated legs, the material catching and tugging like loose strands of steel wool. She pulls on a simple cotton dress, white and stiff and fitted. The collar itches. She selects a gap-toothed plastic comb from a dresser littered with plastic barrettes and polka-dotted ribbons and runs it through her hair, managing at least to make the snags lie flat. She pulls her mother's patent leather shoes over her bare feet. They still shift around past her dirty toenails. Too big, even now.

She lets the screen door rattle in its frame as she steps outside. Rusted wires graze off of her patent leather. The strawberries need watering. The oregano could be weeded. The fertilizer is getting thin in the carrot plots and should be replaced. The trowel and shears lie in the dirt. The woman witches. Sways back and forth. The heavy fabric of her skirt gives ever so slightly to her momentum.

She slowly walks to the edge of the garden, toward the willow branches. The degraded strawberry carcasses are now melded with their tattered thatched basket. The honeydews must be harvested. There will be frost soon. She grabs a branch. A straw broom ponytail winks past her field of vision. Ivy twining around chubby perfect legs. Her grip snaps the branch in half. Her knees knock, about to give way. Another step. And one more.

Amy, I'm so sorry.

She steps over the honeydews, stalks catching on her dress. Drips of salty tears fertilize the ground. Her whole body trembles. She is in motion. The garden beckons to her, but she cannot hear. More willow branches graze her back. A diluted ray of sun strikes her face.

My baby girl.

She rends the shroud of branches in two. The morning sun casts deep shadows over her gaunt face and burns her flesh. She collapses to the ground, her mother's shoes cast from her feet. The neighbors watch her hollow eyes swell as the woman finally lets out a creaking wail that shakes her entire frame.

In the distance, she hears a faint voice.

I love you, mommy.

The Gumby Interview
Tom Luddecke

Editor's Note: This interview was conducted in 1988 and some of the people mentioned or their careers may no longer be alive, which may be a good thing for legal purposes.

Last week it was learned that one-time child star, Gumby had been arrested and charged with three counts of income tax evasion. *Dirty Truth Magazine* caught up with the clay giant at his plush apartment overlooking Park Avenue in New York City. For most of the interview the big green guy was rather serious, but on occasion that rolled clay mouth of his would crinkle up into that familiar Gumby smile.

Dirty Truth: You look good, Gumby, at least as youthful as you did when you were on television.

Gumby: Thanks. Of course, I tend to harden more easily now if I don't exercise regularly, and I've lost a bit of the ability to roll myself up and around like I did on the show, but hey, I'm doing okay.

Dirty Truth: If you don't mind me asking, just how old are you?

Gumby: Well, I'm about the same age as the Beaver, so that should tell you something. By the way, have you seen that guy lately? He looks more like his buddy Larry Mondello. His chin and neck have actually merged into one piece and his crater-filled face looks like it's in a constant state of allergic edema. His teenage years must have been hell, that is, if you can read anyone's face. Ward, I'm worried about the Beaver. Heh, heh.

Dirty Truth: Little harsh, aren't you?

Gumby: Hey, you asked how old I am. I gave you a reference point, you know? I just can't believe how the guy let himself go like that. I mean, could the Beav do this?
(*Gumby's entire bottom half collapses into a plop of clay.*)

Dirty Truth: No, I don't think most of humanity could do that. So, Gumby, I have to ask. What about the income tax evasion charges?

Gumby: A little misunderstanding, a little bad advice. No big deal.

Dirty Truth: So, what happened?

Gumby: Well, I can't go into too much detail because of the legal proceedings. A few years ago I was at a party and heard from a mutual friend that GI Joe didn't pay any taxes on his income. He was exempt for some reason. I guess I assumed it was because he was not human but a doll figure, and I thought I fit into the same mold, no pun intended. Anyway, it turns out the exemption had something to do with his military service and the promotion of American ideals, values, and other such stuff. The bottom line is my lawyer thinks he can work something out.

Dirty Truth: That's good. Other than that, how's the career going now?

Gumby: Pretty good. I don't mind telling you there were some lean years, but ever since Eddie Murray did his Gumby bit on Saturday Night Live I've become more in demand. Some stations are reviving old shows and the residuals are flowing in again.

Dirty Truth: Then you don't feel that this revival is just a cult fad like Betty Boop or something?

Gumby: No, I don't think it's just a fad. I think I'm finally being recognized as a unique talent. I think my show, although it brought me popularity, also typecast me. I mean how many movies are written for a clay hero? Oh, and please don't compare me to Boopsie. All she could do was wiggle and sexually innuendo her way through a cartoon. Mindless gesticulations, that's all.

Dirty Truth: And your clay movements aren't?

Gumby: Look, I've admitted that the show didn't test my abilities, but I have them and that's the difference. And on the show at least I solved some problems and got out of some sticky situations. Boop had a hard time finding her way out of a bathtub without help.

Dirty Truth: Correct me if I'm wrong, but weren't you two an item a while back?

Gumby: I was young. She had been a big celebrity by then. I was star struck. Anyway, it didn't last long. There was no dimension to the relationship, and her voice was on the verge of causing me premature deafness.

Dirty Truth: What did you do after the show went off the air?

Gumby: I toured the country making personal appearances, speaking and performing some tricks like I did on the show.

Dirty Truth: That was some pretty amazing stuff you did. Where did you learn it?

Gumby: Thanks. Most of my training came from my mother. She developed most of the clay transformations, as we called them.

Dirty Truth: Just how did she develop them?

Gumby: Actually it grew out of a hobby of hers. For some unknown reason she was fascinated by cellophane and would collect bags, sheets, wrap, whatever she could get her hands on. Then from time to time she would light the stuff on fire and watch it crumple up into itself. And that's where she got the idea for the clay transformations you saw me do on the show. I would crumple up like that cellophane and then emerge into other shapes.

Dirty Truth: That's incredible. Where is your mother now?

Gumby: She's a product developer at Play-Doh.

Dirty Truth: And your father, did he have any influence on your life?

Gumby: No, my father abandoned us when I was very young. He was pretty much a loner, complaining we were holding him back and that the smell of burning cellophane was killing him. So he took off for the Southwest and became part of an adobe brick commune or something like that.

Dirty Truth: What else have you been doing?

Gumby: Well, after the clay transformations wore thin, I worked some clubs doing stand-up comedy. But it was difficult to be taken seriously as a comedian, if you'll pardon the contradiction in terms. Every time I performed, the audience would heckle me to do my old clay transformations. So I dropped the club appearances to get into other forms of entertainment to demonstrate my diversity as an actor and performer.

Dirty Truth: Such as?

Gumby: I traveled with a theater group production of *Cat on a Hot Tin Roof*, playing Big Daddy.

Dirty Truth: Sounds interesting. Did you bring any of your old transformations to the part?

Gumby: No, not at all, that is, after the first change. I simply remolded myself to the approximate size of Burl Ives and left it like that.

Dirty Truth: How did it go?

Gumby: Truthfully? The critics loved it. But I would still get the hecklers in the audience yelling things like, "Roll into a ball, Gumby!" or "C'mon, Big Daddy, stretch yourself to that hot tin roof!" Things like that. It was very discouraging.

Dirty Truth: What are you doing now?

Gumby: I formed my own production company, *Chicken Gumbo Products*, and I'm writing, directing, and producing short documentaries with an eye toward movies later.

Dirty Truth: What are some of the documentaries you have done?

Gumby: Well, I'm very proud of my most recent one and have high hopes for its success. It's about the life and death spawning struggle of the Atlantic salmon and it's entitled, *The Atlantic Salmon – Let's Try an Easier Way*. It documents the efforts of a marine life group as they retrain the instinctive habits of the Atlantic salmon. They are attempting to get the fish to spawn near the mouth of the river. It would save them a lot of grief and increase their survival rate. There has been some controversy with the Greenpeace group, which claimed the efforts were disrupting the natural process of selective breeding and survival of the fittest. They believed that this would eventually prove harmful to the salmon by producing inferior offspring. I mean talk about your Aryan philosophy or what? Those guys should be shuttled to unknown galaxies. Rainbow Warrior space travelers, heh, heh, saviors of interplanetary world life, heh. Probably get devoured by some frenzied Plutonian endangered species.

Dirty Truth: Gumby, I think we're a bit off the topic.

Gumby: Sorry.

Dirty Truth: How was it working with Pokey?

Gumby: Pokey was very hard to work with on the set. Things had to be just right with that critter.

Dirty Truth: Do you still see or hear from him?

Gumby:	Only once. He wanted to get together for some reunion performances.
Dirty Truth:	What happened?
Gumby:	I turned him down. We parted on bad terms. He wanted a bigger cut of the residuals from the show. He felt he was as much the star as I was. I reminded him what the name of the show was and who taught him about the clay transformation tricks. He left kind of ticked off.
Dirty Truth:	Do you know what he is doing now?
Gumby:	He's a businessman now or business horse I guess you would say. He owns some company that disposes of ground clutter; you know that stuff that constantly shows up on those weather radar maps.
Dirty Truth:	What are your plans for the future?
Gumby:	I knew you would ask that and I was prepared to say something humorous, such as, I'd like to write technical manuals, play major league baseball, or perform arcane experiments on armadillos. But I'm in a more serious frame of mind now.
Dirty Truth:	So?
Gumby:	Well, I'm finishing filming my own exercise video, *Gumby's Workout for Stiffs*. I use the clay transformation theory as the basis of the exercise format. Of course I moderate it so humans can simulate the exercises. In the future I'd also like to produce and direct feature-length movies.
Dirty Truth:	If you could change one thing in you life, past or present, what would it be?
Gumby:	I think I'd wrap G.I. Joe in cellophane and call my mother.
Dirty Truth:	Thank you, Gumby.
Gumby:	My pleasure.

For Anyone Interested
Richard Luftig

It is March and I realize
that you nuthatches and martins,
towhees and longspurs
down in Florida have evidently
not gotten the memo about
the cheap rents available
in the Indiana trees
that can be had for a song.

But I am here, a self-appointed
proxy of spring, taking out ads
in the Miami papers and vying
for airtime on Tampa talk shows
just to clue in any random
waxwings that might tune in
that wooly hemlocks up north
are shedding their stiff coats,

and shaking the snow off
their firs while the boxelders
and blackjack oaks are eager
to display their new pretenses
of leaves. But beware:
this Public Service Announcement
is first-come-first-served,
an Early Bird Special of sorts

no rain checks issued and made
on behalf of your cooped- up,
cabin-fevered, prairie friends
and neighbors who are still stuck
inside, frantically addressing
to you idyllic picture postcards,
filled in with pleading messages,
of *we wish you were here.*

First Snow
Richard Luftig

Cut out of white paper
and taped on the inside

of the second floor window
window of a kindergarten class.

There are names under each one:
Raul, Melinda, Paulina, Gabe.

From below in the schoolyard,
no two exist exactly alike.

Carrying My Pants
April Salzano

I carry my pants
up and down the steps
all night. I begin downstairs, pants off,
in my own bed with my husband at 9 p.m.
Somewhere around midnight, pants on,
upstairs in bed with a crying
son. It's hard to comfort him in just underwear.
He slides his jagged toenails up and down
my legs, which he insists on intertwining
with his own, one hand on my neck, crowding
me and taking the lion's share of the pillow.
I sneak back downstairs, remove my pants
and slip into memory
foam mattress, under down
comforter. Pants on, up
the stairs, pants off, down
at 2 a.m. When summoned again,
I just grab puddle of pants
from one bedroom floor and relocate it
to another. I repeat this dysfunctional
striptease until light comes
to rescue me. I don't know which room
I am in and I cannot find my pants.

Destinations
William Odgen Haynes

Masks on tubes suddenly bloom
like upside-down buttercups.
Acrid smoldering of electrical wiring
hangs a thin haze over the cabin.
A flight attendant's mouth is drawn
into a razor slit as the fuselage torques,
opening the clasps of overhead compartments
allowing carry-ons to pop out
like untethered Jacks in a box.
The overhead lights dim, then extinguish,
and ribbons of light embedded
in the floor illuminate fallen
coats and bags in the center aisle.

He didn't know the young woman
in the window seat,
her head covered with a blue *hijab*.
They were bound together
only by the serendipity
of seat assignment.
But they reached out at the same time,
grasping hands across the armrest.
She smiled at him and said
over the roar of engines,
"Today I will be in paradise."
And his last thought was
that he couldn't even
make it to Chicago.

Woody
Michael J. Soloway

Summer was a crazy uncle, an easygoing grandparent, a substitute teacher. It gave us permission, permission to do things we wouldn't do in any other season or at any other time of year or under so-called normal circumstances. It made us take our BB guns into the woods and shoot things. *Pump. Pump. Pump.* It convinced us to drag our bikes through the dirt and leaves and downed branches so we could blow up our flat tires until they felt like rubber mallets. *Pump. Pump. Pump.* And when we got bored and daring enough, we did more boy things, like exterminate ant hills with our feet, climb trees, or even masturbate, on a tree stump, into a pile of brush, or a stagnant brook that ran the length of our development and had a few Brim but no other life to speak of, except mosquito larvae and green algae. *Pump. Pump. Pump.*

Summer was built for change and as an outlet for our fears. It was sports and turning sprinkler heads so they soaked wooden fences and concrete patios instead of scorched grass. It was shooting birds, both figuratively and literally. Pigeons mostly. Stupid and low-flying, they made their way into the woods by accident and now couldn't find their way out. We saw to it to put them out of their misery. We felt it was our responsibility so we stockpiled CO_2 cartridges and pumped up our guns past the recommended rates. *Pump. Pump. Pump.*

We did things other people—adults—would be arrested for, and thought it was our natural right. *Summer was our Constitution, scribbled in pencil, rewritten every day, until school buses started running again, and teachers forced us to put our summers on loose-leaf paper, summaries full of lies and exaggerations.* We had fantasies and delusions of grandeur. We imagined we were a gang of the last remaining human beings on earth, the woods a deserted island to explore and pillage. Rocks were both weapons and toys. Branches were swords and canes and a way to write profanities in mud. Girls didn't exist. Birds were prey. We thought we'd build a fire and eat them, even if our mothers tried to break this spell by calling us home for dinner.

Summer put us in the woods with animals. Squirrels. Pigeons. Snakes. Lizard. Deer. Each other. Once, Richie Briggs, who we all called "Little Richie," because of a glandular problem, claimed he saw a black panther. We were convinced he saw Alfred, a cat from the neighborhood, which at twenty-three pounds had its own glandular problems.

Summer was also freedom, catching lizards and putting them in mason jars, thunderstorms that materialized over the ocean, and choking on the weight of the Florida humidity. We would all sweat more and average three showers a day. It was scaring ourselves for the high, by walking through the cemetery; it was spending longer days in the sun, as well as finding shade, wherever it seemed to land—underneath the Spanish moss of a live oak, in a neighbor's garage, or an abandoned fort or cabin. That's why it happened in the first place. We were looking for a break, a shelter; we were looking for shade and a way out of the rain.

Summer was peer pressure pushing us further into the brush than we had ever gone before. One day, we came upon a shack. Wooden with a metal roof. The rust an orange beacon, a sure sign to turn back. A drizzle had started to flit against the shadows and a fickle sun. The rain tapped leaves, like BBs shot straight up into the air and back to earth, dusting our heads with water. Harder. Larger. Faster. On the tin roof. *Summer was taking shelter in the cabin and waiting for the rain to pass.*

Inside the shack were sharp edges: hedge clippers, a broken bat with chards jetting out, a pine table that needed sanding, an aluminum trough for bathing. Everything was capable of cutting you into a million little pieces. Even a calendar nailed to the wall would leave you with a nasty paper cut, if not handled properly, gently, taking care not to tear. I stood there and stared at the accumulations of a life. We wondered who lived there and when they would return. An old man, someone said. A bum. A child molester. A one-eyed monster.

Although the special calendar was visible from every corner of the shack, we three huddled around the month of May—"Michele" on the bow of a boat, her boobs exposed, hanging, touching the white fiberglass with her nipples. I remember the color of her hair—brown—because it was the only thing visible besides flesh. Besides my mom, I had never seen a naked woman before. It felt bad and wrong to me. But we all scrambled to see her, and pushed and pointed our guns at each other for a better view. Then Big Richie found a stack of magazines in the corner, every month of *Playboy* from 1968 to 1980. Everybody grabbed one, except for Little Richie and me. We stayed with Michele until our eyes wouldn't open any larger. We kept ourselves close while the rest of our boys went to their own corners to kneel on the dirt floor.

I hadn't considered stealing from the old man until that moment, with seventh grade behind me, and the threat of another summer alone with my mother hanging over me. I wasn't a thief. The only thing I had ever taken was a pack of bubble gum from a drugstore when I was four. My mother made me return it and apologize to the manager. That was before she beat me in plain sight. In fact, I don't know what made want to rip off the old man. Perhaps it was the weight of the south Florida humidity covering my mouth with its heavy hand. Perhaps it was just Little Richie staring at her with his hands down his pants, his woody testing his short's zipper.

I left my gun but Michele was coming with me. I grabbed her off the wall. I ran. Sprinted. I wanted to move in a straight line and leave all this behind. Keep moving. Move your little legs. *Pump. Pump. Pump.* Run. *Pump. Pump. Pump.* Run and hide. Find your way out. Don't be a pigeon. *Pump. Pump. Pump.* Move those skinny legs. Through the rain. Or was it BBs at my back?

Summer was wanderlust, Michele, Miss May. Summer was never having to look back. Summer was a BB gun. Shot, it might sting for a minute. But it wouldn't kill you. Summer would fill you up like a helium balloon. Change your voice. Make you float through the trees. *Summer would leave its mark. Pump. Pump. Pump.*

Miss May would stay with me for years. Eighth grade. In high school. Even when faded and ripped and lost for good, she would still be there, imprinted in me like an image on a worn computer screen. I would carry her into college, into relationships, and eventually into marriages. She would make me feel small, like Little Richie. Summer was a merry-go-round and I wanted to get off. I never had a nickname like the Richies, but that day was coming, as sure as a Florida thunderstorm, as sure as June would follow May. I felt it. It was just a mist in my hair and on my tongue, but I still felt it, and that's no exaggeration.

summer stanzas
Changming Yuan

June

Come, come to the open fields
Let's embrace most daylight
Of the whole year
In this northern hemisphere
Where we can stay young, younger
Enjoying our honeymoon
With the sun, with light
With warmth
Instead of cold darkness
That is dominating the other
Half of the world

July

Dogs are making human history (right)
When humans deal with dog days (right)
When the sullen, sultry sky witnesses:
Fraud, fervor, frenzy -- yes
It is our inner heat that has been
Warming the whole atmosphere
Like Julius's inflated heart

August

With stone fruits
Like plums, apricots, preaches
Ripening rapidly
In this month of the sickle
It is high time to cut open
The secrets of sunlight
In their hardened hearts
Wrapped with the fleshiest
The juiciest season

You might forget that I know too
Dana Green

You will be the only person to know what will happen, someone we will never meet will know why.

--

I found a list of things that will disappear when something bad happens. Number one-hundred is goats/chickens. There are only one hundred listed, after one hundred everything disappears. You said that the bad thing that starts the disappearing is the ninety-second most likely bad thing. The cement will be cracked uneven, when people run for their lives they will trip but continue.

--

We will talk about things and decide that we will keep chickens in the basement and goats on the front lawn, sometimes you will stop remembering why. I will make a graph showing when the world will end and you will draw a pie chart. Our findings will make us believe that the bad thing will be in our lifetime. Everything will continue job weekend normal. I still want children. You might be okay with that.

--

Sometimes things get too much and something needs to happen. Something happens and the world does not. You told me that it is ninety-five percent likely the world will stop spinning when it ends. There is a law that says that everything will move place when the world breaks that fast. You said that somewhere they have a list of most likely events, objects, and people that will change the rotation. I think that when the world ends the world does not need to stop, but I do not know if I am someone to trust.

--

Our house is nailed everywhere. You will buy me a nail gun instead of jewelry. We keep duct tape in our bags for when things get insecure. We will promise each other to keep the end of the world secret, it will make us feel guilty in our stomachs but you said it is best not to worry people. Also, we have seen what the world does to people who warn of the end.

--

Last night I dreamt you forgot what was going to happen.

--

The world will not end even though everyone will die when the world ends. I think there will be only one airplane in the air, most likely full of kind-hearted humans. All of the women will be pregnant. Something that has to do with what caused the bad thing to happen will not be able to reach the airplane. It will be high up hiding softly in clouds. When the airplane lands the passengers will cry as long as they need to then begin to build houses out of. I do not know if I will end with the world or not.

--

I ask you to tell me that everything will be okay. You say that we will see what we will, what we can.

hung   V. Smith

LAUNDRY LINES

Our Clothesline
AJ Huffman

doubled as a run for the dog
in winter. Waving sheets and towels replaced
by wagging tail and trailing chain,
back and forth along the length of fraying
rope. It was too hard to chase
our aging Collie through snow that was always waist
deep. He lopped through it as if he was
weaving through the sun-drying fabric of summer,
mother yelling at him to *get back*
because *those are clean*. In his brilliant brown eyes,
the temperature did not matter, only the wind
against his face as he flew.

Jeopardy
Lisa Fusch Krause

So much like growing up—
giving up my reality
for a freshly starched new one
handcrafted by my mother

I'm washed clean,
as if my mom
mixed me with the laundry

Darks cold, whites hot,
and iron everything
No one spots a wrinkle;
nothing wrong is ever seen

Mom, you coughed up blood
on that trip to California
My sister and I weren't told

Was there a reason
you watched "Jeopardy"
while ironing?

Was there?

Out to Dry
April Salzano

Our backyard clothesline was a testament
to poverty that persisted through my childhood. Panties
waved to the neighbors, little white flags that increased
in size and number as three girls reached puberty.
Later, they hung on the middle line, their rust-colored
crotch stains carefully obscured by placement—
never hung inside out, always flanked by denim
or towels. I was all spite and resentment when
take the clothes off the line was on my chore list.
I never folded,
the towels stiff with sunshine,
the jeans ungiving against frantic shaking. I hurled
everything in the basket waiting under the last garment
my mother had hung that morning.
I threw the clothespins in the yard to be spit back
by lawnmower blades, chewed and useless.
We had a dryer, but *sunshine is free*,
my mom chanted, a generation beyond
the Great Depression. Winter brought reprieve.
She wasn't that die-hard for outdoor freshness,
an oxymoron in a town that allowed leaf and garbage
burning. As an adult, my underwear properly
treated with advancements in stain removal,
I admit to having considered hanging a line,
guilted by green propaganda and the wish
for a lower electric bill, but I cannot seem to
bring myself to walk back along a path
landmarked by the necessity of humiliation.

Lights and Darks
Rosemary Jones

She's downstairs sorting the washing. Underwear and socks. Shirts . Jeans. Lights and darks. Etceteras. Today she does his separately, so they won't soil hers, or the children's. She scoops up a sour bundle tossing them into the machine with more force than usual. Pours in the soap, chooses the setting, listens for the rush of water before she clicks the bathroom door shut, returning to the living room to sit by the window, all other chores forgotten. The sky hasn't been blue for days. But a patch of it sails by as if it's just pulled in from somewhere else. Ready and waiting to take her wherever she chooses.

What she chooses is another time in another country, at home on a spring day when pollen released from silver wattle trees floats in the air, and she's hanging out the washing on her mother's Hill's Hoist clothes line. She pegs a man's shirt by the tail so it will blouse out, flapping like a man on the run. She shakes out a pair of underpants with a hard thwack and clips them to the line. The wooden pegs stand upright in a row, doll-like, weather worn. Orderly. A measured dance.

She conjures other things: the cane washing basket, drained of its original color, turned to silver: the green grass under her feet: the blue sky above, a light, expansive blue. And then there's the walk back to the house under the eaves to the verandah. The gentle slam of the back door, a task completed. Sometimes as a teenager she might sit with a cup of coffee in the back garden, reading on the sun-warmed concrete path up to the back fence beside exuberances of parsley, sweet peas, a trellis of green beans. Her father's subtractions and additions of vegetable plots, flower beds, herb patches. As a child, she and her siblings each had a small garden in a raised bed above a half circumference stone wall that fanned around the clothes line. Carrots mainly. The soil got under her nails. The snails feasted on the tops. The clothes dried in the breeze above.

Hanging out the family's washing is a memory that will keep playing in her head whatever happens. Arms extended up to the line. Her fingers scrabbling for pegs. The clatter of the wheels of the washing basket cart rolling down the grassy knoll, then hitting the brick paving before gliding over the smooth concrete of the back verandah. Magpies wardling. The postman on his motor bike, stopping at each letter box, before revving the engine and going full speed along the footpath to the next house.

She wants things back the way they were. Pines for them. Bites her nails for them, a new habit. Through the door, she hears the washing machine shift from a regular chug to the frantic pace of the spin cycle.

Her husband is having an affair. She had thought so. The idea would pop into her head as ridiculous at first, rolling around like a loose colored marble. Then it would roll away. Unaccountably, it would roll back. She asked him and he denied it, more than once, until he blurted it out to her one night and the world stopped. It didn't stop as it did when she hung the washing on the line, her arms outstretched in a serene muscular action. It stopped as if the postman had screeched to a halt at the front gate and run over a child; she heard the shock of his brakes, a jagged child scream. He says that he has to find the truth of the matter. He is deciding which one he will choose. Really, men don't have enough time at the washing line, she thinks.

Her second favorite washing line was trucked in from the city over eight hundred kilometers into the desert where it was planted in the dusty pink sandy soil of her front yard. A green stalk with squares of yellow line spinning around like the spokes of an umbrella in hot, dry winds. She thinks about the forays from her dug-out, an underground dwelling cut out of sandstone, the washing basket tucked under her arm as she walked into a wall of heat. Or hot nights under the stars pegging and un-pegging at the line. It makes her giddy. A different kind of pleasure. As if she had been brave enough then to climb into a rocket and shoot off to live on the outer rim of the moon. Burrowing in like a miner into the side of a hill. Chipping out a shelf for flour and tea and sugar. Caressing her moon walls like a lover's hair. Sniffing the yellow. Breathing in the color, the blaze of it. She was close enough to the moon then, it hovered at the end of the front yard like a nightly visitor. Bold-faced some nights. Eyes guarded at others, hiding behind a veil of rain-empty clouds.

She wonders what it will be like when her husband chooses and how he might make the announcement. Perhaps he'll put it in the paper like a notice of a canceled engagement. She thinks if she is not chosen she will be relieved, relieved from living forever with the knowledge that he did this and trying to pretend that he didn't. All those fake smiles she'll have to put on. All those everything-is-perfectly-fine conversations, when in reality something dark, like the rumbling sound of an air-bomber rises and falls through her days.

In the beginning he used to brush her hair. It fell to her shoulders and as he brushed he hummed, as if he were strolling down a European street to buy fresh bread and a round of cheese. Or pastries. At least, that's how the hum sounded, both hopeful and satisfied as the bristles pressed firmly into her scalp and electricity caused some of the hairs on the top of her head to fly upwards. At the core of this hair-brushing happiness, sat a small light circle, like a lucky charm. Now life had more strands to it. Like strings of metal weighing down her neck. And the lucky charm of happiness, his, hers, had shrunk to a small discardable thing, as if someone had left it on a shelf, and then kept moving it, and she couldn't keep track of its exact location. She wondered if her husband stroked the new woman's hair, Geraldine's hair, and if so whether he was trying to reactivate a younger self. Find a pool of light in himself. And whether what he saw in her, as his wife, had shrunk to that of fetcher and carrier. A figure at the washing line.

Alas, now there is no washing line. Their apartment is complete with washer and dryer in the bathroom. So she is always bending her back over it, sticking her head in the dryer, hauling out clothes, stuffing them back in. It isn't the same. There isn't the smell of air on them, or desert sun, or the leafy scent from a suburban back garden.

Before the apartment, before life in this new country, one of her washing lines had been planted in a dusty, reddened back yard next to a couple of brave eucalyptus trees in soil so sandy it was a wonder anything took root. Lawn didn't. Occasionally pig-face, the succulent ground-cover did. On windy days the sand whipped up, left streaks on the white sheets. The pegs got grit in them. Washing and drying was harder work. It rained more often there on the edge of the desert than it had in the dry desert center. It was a sort of in between land. In between city and country. Sure, they called where she lived a city, but it was a city that abruptly stopped as if it had forgotten about its self and its periphery because when you went walking in it the next thing you knew you were striding out into salt bush and blue bush. In between land and sea. On the edge of a gulf, where the mangroves stank and the beaches were often beset by low tide. In between desert and farmland, though the farmland was miles away.

Despite the in betweeness, she would have rewound time and gone back there. She was more innocent then. Not all that innocent, but innocent by comparison. Free from the dark metallic shapes of airplanes flying in formation towards her. She knows nothing about planes. Or war paraphernalia or how much damage can be done with weaponry but she thinks now that if her husband chooses Geraldine, she might want to shoot him. Poor Geraldine, she wouldn't have him for long. No scenes of domestic bliss for her.

They are bad thoughts. A woman doing her washing is meant to think of tonight's casserole, tomorrow's sick child, or if she is an artist, what colors to squeeze onto her palette. If she could play with time, if she were the one who had extracted this prize piece of information, the fact of his adultery, and held it aloft like a victory cup, then the balance of power might have shifted. He might have been impressed. Hmm, not bad, he might have thought. She's worth it. But he had been too shifty, and she too trusting.

It is a problem. The dark metallic objects. Even now, out the window slicing through the little patch of blue, they keep making themselves known, shouting interjections. Black humps of anger. She wishes she could grab hold of them and throw them high over a back fence, away from the vision of her washing lines.

It's good then that she doesn't have to hang out her husband's washing – shirts, underpants, socks. They'll merely go round and round in the dryer. Pegging each piece of his clothing would be an intimacy, a free-fall imagining of his density and the tender places underneath. Now she would want to rip his underpants to shreds, peg what was left of them grimly on the line for the rest of the summer to fade, a humiliation, in summer rains. She'd want to snip out the shape of a heart in his favorite shirt and leave the hole gaping. She would hang it, freshly starched and ironed in his closet, ready for his next rendezvous with Geraldine.

There is something to be said for small acts of vengeance. Like little acts of love, but in reverse, they signify equivalence. What has been taken away. She thinks she hears the faint roar of engines; almost out of the frame of the window pane, she catches a high gleam of metal turning into the sun in the patch of blue sky. Like an eagle. Watchful, like big wedge-tail eagles that used to squat on the desert roads, picking over kangaroo road kill. Tearing at the meat. Reluctant to leave the tender morsels as she drove highway-fast along the road towards one. It invariably waited for the last minute, eyeing her, before painstakingly unfolding its wings and flying off, belly-heavy, flapping out of her collision course just in time. She begins to make a list of vengeful acts. When they are completed she will cross them off, one by one.

It's possible her mother cried at the washing line. In those small, snatched windblown moments, she too must have thought about her life. Reckoning its list of shortcomings, defeats. Or perhaps standing there, pegging, un-pegging, may have offered a respite. Like staring into a rock pool searching for starfish, miniature darts of color. She wishes she could ask her, but her mother cannot advise her now; she is far away, imagining her daughter in another world, a larger, stranger world. But not a formidable world, not a world of sorrow, no, she would not be imagining that. In the late afternoon she will phone her; she will yell loudly into the receiver to the other side of the world, and tell her that she misses her, although the sound of her yelling something that should be said *sotto voce*, will embarrass her. Her mother will be puzzled and not realizing what it is about will ask when she's bringing the family home. And the sound of love will clatter over the Pacific Ocean. A solace. Almost the smell of home.

Once she mentioned to him that she missed her washing lines on the other side of the world, how removed from herself she felt without one, but he had only extolled the virtues of modern technology. He had not understood what she'd given up.

The washing machine has clunked to a halt. She rises to attention. Back to work. As she pulls out his underwear and shoves it up into the dryer, she imagines she has returned, not to the desert, but to her mother's washing line again. Instead of being a young girl at the line while her brothers whooped around in her peripheral vision, one of them swinging dangerously off the end of a corner of the Hill's Hoist, she is as she is now. She is hanging out her husband's and her children's clothes. American jeans and chinos and t-shirts with now familiar names that once she'd never heard of. With a load of American washing in front of her, she rakes the basket for Australian pegs. The back lawn smells of fresh grass clippings. Far off in the distance drones the sound of someone's lawn mower. A flock of pink galahs fly above, squawking for fruit. The Hill's Hoist squeaks a little as it turns on its thick, metal axis. She pegs the wet washing, spins the line around, pegs again. And then without warning a rod of anger fires up her legs through her spine. She pitches forward to hold the trunk of the Hill's Hoist. She grips the metal, pressing her body into it, and the metal seems to steady her as she shouts into the Australian sky. She pauses for a barely a second to gather up more saliva and out spills a stream of invectives.

After the shouting is over, she sinks into the grass. A wind catches the line so it turns, squeaks, turns again. Her head is bent over her knees. It's from that position she hears the ponderous flap of a wedge-tail eagle flying in to squat beside her. Come to tug at her innards? Sit on her one of her arms as if it were a branch? With both hands she shoos it off. But her limbs go heavy, encased by the sensation of wings. Warrior feathers prickle her face. Stately, long feathers in earthy browns and blacks. She catches her breath. Trance-like she stands and throws in a load of darks. Bangs down the lid of the washing machine.

When she returns to the living room, the patch of blue out the window sails away taking with it the Hill's Hoist, the smell of her Australian back yard, but not the wings. It's as if someone has sewn them on while she wasn't looking. They drape like curtains. She can feel them wanting to flutter ever so gently when she tries to lift them out of the way of the furniture. As if a flock of birds has banded together and donated them. It isn't clear to her how long she will wear these wings of sorrow, but they are now her companions, both a burden and a gift sent from her washing line day dreams. There is comfort in their heft, their rustling, dark bush colors. She has to stand straighter because of them. She knows when she opens the door to her husband, although she may appear heavier, she will also be more earthed. She isn't going to fly away, though she could, the wings could open out and spread into a wide, awkward span. She could take off clumsily from the roof and circle the city in bigger and bigger arcs until she gets the hang of the air currents. But she won't. The key is turning in the lock. That's him now. The wings propel her toward the door, like a bird skimming across a lake. She doesn't speak to him, and she doesn't smile; wedge-tail eagles are not that kind of bird. She fastens her metallic, hooded eyes on him, and blinks at the oncoming shape.

Laundry Bees and the Swish of Skirts
C. Beth Loofe

There is something strong...safe, about a sturdy post and wire. They offer security. Boundaries. Communication. When our country was young, cattlemen protested as wire and posts barbed their way like patchwork parcels piercing across a country that used to be open range. Not so long after, these same men were unadmittedly grateful their stock was kept safer from thieves and other predators, would the cattle have been allowed to ramble. It wasn't foolproof, but it helped. Not much later, other posts and wires were sprouting on the grasslands, telegraph evolving into telephone wires, joining one coast to another with an almost instant relay of information.

But these tall pine sentries, connected over the miles, weren't the first ones to communicate news and gossip to all who needed to know it, nor was barbed wire the first line to keep a community's interests protected. Before I was old enough to know about cattlemen warring with sheep herders or Alexander Graham Bell and his predecessors, I knew about the *first* posts and wires. They were as much a part of my tradition and my history as my name.

I grew up in a small town; one and a half square miles, one hundred and five people, two ways in and a two fingered wave pretty much summed it up. Everyone had a telephone, but back then it was 'long distance' to call the 'big city' ten miles to the south, so not many did. And no one called each other. You talked at the post office, at church, or at the clothes line.

The clothes line was an important thing. You were judged by it, though no one said so. If yours was rusty and bent, wives, tsked-tsked, sucked their teeth and whispered behind their hands, and the owner's back, about how disgraceful it was that her husband couldn't do better by her. Then to her face, offered polite smiles and asked about the children and the weather. Women who hung their clothes on those umbrella type laundry lines didn't fair much better. They were considered an eyesore, and worse yet, how could one share information over an umbrella? It just didn't have the necessary ergonomic dynamic that was needed.

Our clothes line was stately. It seemed seventy feet long, but in reality was only twenty. Tall, straight and pointing toward the sun with arms outstretched. It had not just three lines, but four. It was green first, for a long while and then later silver, and never, ever rusty. Nestled in the center of the back yard, it was flanked by the stark white garage on one side, the wood pile and propane tank on the other. The house and giant garden brought up the ends. Even though the ancient pine and mulberry trees towered nearby, I never remember any evidence of the birds that must have lived in them on the wash that hung underneath.

Yes, our clothesline was a thing to be proud of in a small town where pride was something to confess on Saturday nights, but still, my grandmother beamed. No one talked about the weather, or asked- too intently- about me when they came to visit. What they did ask about were the important things. Contrary to small town stereotype and myth, these women were not gossip filled hens cackling about Betty's fallen cake or Marge's yellowed sheets. Well, sometimes they were, but more often than not these women, in spite the occasional sucked teeth hidden behind a judging hand, organized prayer chains and casserole bakes for the injured farmer and his family, 'cleaning committees' for the newly widowed neighbor mired in too much grief to take care of the house work herself and figured out ways their husbands could cajole *her* husband into doing better. And not just by way of a new clothesline.

These women were a sisterhood. Not just a sorority, woven in cottons and linen bound by wood pegs over steel, but by work and trust and time. No woman seemed to do their wash on the same day at the same hour. Although I accepted this as just the way it was, I didn't understand it until well into my adulthood. At the age of thirty-two while visiting home and driving by a former neighbor's wash floating on the wire, it suddenly made sense to me that if two or more lines were busy, of course the women couldn't gather all together. As a child, it just seemed normal.

And it was normal that five, seven, sometimes seventeen or more women gathered in a backyard enjoying company and folding, sharing information and fellow...female...ship. Not all the women worked. The task would have been completed in four minutes had that been the case. The old women sat in woven lawn chairs or metal arm loungers painted bright shades of blue or yellow-the favorite colors of bees- drinking lemonade and tending the little girls and babies. The older girls quietly mirrored their mothers, learning how to hang denim so creases would form, and softer cotton so that it wouldn't. And listening to their elders talk, learning how to Be.

I was one of the little girls. Rotating from yard to yard, day to day with my grandmother for the laundry bee's, I could hardly wait to get there even though I was never sure where the 'there' was when we started out. It didn't really matter, since the faces were the same. Only the clothes line was different. Mine...my grandmother's...was still my favorite, naturally.

It was an item of utility, a means of communication but it was also one of the safest places I knew. The smell of sunshine infused in cloth, pressed up against my young face promised forever. If sunshine could be captured like that, then *any* good thing could be held in the palm of a child's hand for eternity. The comforting rustle of laundry on the line could only be outdone by the swish of the skirts of the women whose knees I clung to. Conservative, liberal and religious lines were mixed in regard to apparel in my small town. My grandmother was a strict Catholic, skirt wearing Democrat. Many others were adherent Lutheran skirt wearing Republicans. At least that was true in regard to the older women. And some of the younger ones. In a town which didn't get 'cablevision' until the late 80's and then only briefly, it is not surprising skirts were a predominant choice. The swish of those garments was like wind through pine needles, a soft song, a baby's sigh. That portable sunshine steeped in cloth, and that swish was a guarantee that everything was going to be alright. At least for that moment.

Forty years later, I don't have a clothesline. Although there is space, it's not a popular choice in town. I am not so sure the city birds would be so polite. My sunshine is trapped in a bottle. It smells false and counterfeit. Mostly because it is. No one bothers with creases any more. Permanent press has come and gone. Now even 'wash and wear' is wearing thin in fashion trends and skirts are saved for runway couture and not backyard laundry bee's. And I am not sure when the last time was I talked to my neighbor.

Telephone wires, where they still exist, are largely buried underground. Cell phones use the sky to broadcast information and the internet sends data around the world in the blink of an eye or faster. And clotheslines? Even in the city I see them once in a while, ironically caged in by tall boarded fences, allowing no opportunities for communication, sisterhood or the soft swish of...anything.

Signs
Katherine MacCue

We're not looking for a man
to help us with our laundry.
Laundry. Laundress. Seamstress.
Sensors bins. We bend
into bins
and prick out fingers
on pins.

She says Katha, she can't pronounce
my full name. Likewise, I can't pronounce hers.
Sometimes at night while I'm watching CNN,
infomercials abound on systems and CDs that teach you
a new language in as little as a week. It may deliver but I prefer
to come into work with the intent of being humbled by the rolling of letters
and the light lisp that comes after *grasias*.
I've told her so much without ever
speaking a sentence,
words worked through
the typical way:
subject verb object.

Instead, we smile at each other
and wave our hands assiduously
 to say
goodbye.

Some mornings, she will
tap me on the shoulder
 and lift her arms,
rolls them out
like fresh linen signifying
the dust that collects on mannequin shirts
seething in overhead lighting. I mimic
a similar motion, and it's understood.
The shirts must be fluffed.

The efforts of our hands,
hands of women sitting together in a
stockroom sewing circle
needling our fingers into the garments,
bending and moving and twisting to make
each daily thread meet,

it can be so full, so full
of yolk and conversation.
Pfff, George. No,no! she says

shaking her head in dismay as she scoops
up ten wrinkled shirts from the floor and places them
into the steaming apparatus;
it's the boy who makes her
sweep the floor for a full hour
some days because he cant get a grin
out of her—she recognizes
his hands hold no power to thread.
Pffft, George. No.

I Am No Timid Electra
Katherine MacCue

Hands. We fill buckets
with them, full of raspberries.
My father knew her by them:
stained and scarred from
apologies that made hot pies,
tarts, puckered lips that got
wiped with the edge of a shirt.

Red. My father witnessed the color
of his mother's heart from a knife
his father used for cutting apples,
and prying the lids off of preserves.
She could not be saved from his wrath.

Love. Knowing the thorns
that catch – worth the price
for a cup of summer harvest,
my father still plants his
dreams in rows and,

beaten red by the sun,
puts ointment on
his skin which drizzles
down his back like tear streaks.

Whisper. I used to cry
thinking about it: what
sound does the ache take
on? When, as a child, the thorns
caught my finger, my
father would hold the mouth
of the wound and gently speak to it, saying: there there, let it bleed, let it bleed like this.

Milk
Katherine MacCue

I think of my mother, passing
it through her body to my own,
the small opening I grasped between
my boney gums then let go of as she
tucked herself back in with her hands,
her hands which were the most
persuasive,

with their soft rivulets of
skin and vein unclinching
a clothes pin or pressing down
on a serrated edge through

cucumber sweat. My father never
hung his own clothes to dry or cooked
his own food, never saw the leftover
fluff of dessert accumulate in the corners
of my mouth, little white splinters
that she wiped away with the edge
of a dinner napkin. In the

early years we were full of hectic pace,
moving from state to state, but it was
not my father who heard the sound
of an ax stabbing through the bark of
a young oak tree, the pierce and guttural
punch like a tiny fist to a pillow. It was
my mother who smoothed the wrinkles
of my dress over as as we dropped keys
on doorsteps, left little girls

in long fishtail braids standing
pigeon-toed in the middle of a
cul-de-sac and she would
paint with watercolor their little girl
names over and over on my
eyelids when I could not sleep
in our old new houses. She whispered

familiarity, the constant sun in
my ears, or newness: the arch of
a rainbow that ended gently as initials
on my forehead. She always knew

that I had fallen from some high above
place when I'd come home to tell her,
nodding her head as she poured vinegar

onto my bloodied clothes, a clairvoyance
that I saw as steam rising from an iron
which soothed the scratch of khaki,
like baby oil on parched skin.

 My father, the slam of the front door,
shook his head in disbelief at my
scrapes, not knowing yet how I would
fall again and again. In the steam of

each summer's rolling boil my mother
hung our dreams outside, all of it
glistening off of her amethyst skin,
winking through the spaces between
the weight of wet bedsheets, tying
her hair up in a bun and letting my
lithe body dangle in night's enveloping
darkness from the thin clothesline, the
thin wire that held up sheets, shirts,
different fabrics all the color of milk,
the color of what my mother passed
from her bosom to my breath saying,
here is the light, here it is,
inside our bodies.

At the Fiddle Contest, 1926
Lynn Pruett

"Church is different, Dora," Pa said. "Everybody's got their mouth open and everybody's looking at God." He pushed back from his plate, waiting. The oil cloth hilled up where his elbows had been. I resisted my need to smooth it out.

Instead, I put a slice of cheddar on top of his peach pie. "Remember Leola got stranded by the war."

So here we are, viewing the prizes on stage, a pair of cotton socks, bib, Pa's size, a sack of flour, and two green dollar bills clipped together like husband and wife. Pa holds my hand. They never let a girl sing before. The crowd will love Leola like Pa and I do.

I hope there's a mirror backstage. Leola's hair's wild and yellow as dandelions. Mine's silver strands among the gold. Pa's is all gray. It looks like combed metal.

If we win the two dollars, if Leola wins the two dollars, Pa ca drop it in the collection plate on Sunday. But I don't say this. I don't want to jinx Leola.

Two boys are playing guitars but I like a whole band.

I often dream of Leola being swept to the altar on a hymn, stepping free of Pa's arm, me and the kinfolk smiling. Just like Mellie Ivy is smiling now, way up front strapped in a new calico, prowling.

The boys are singing high harmony:

Two old maids playin' in the sand
Each one wishin' the othern was a man

I like a whole band like Leola has behind her, a banjo, the fiddle high and slow and mournful, a bass to thump like frogs in the spring. A guitar strumming, strumming like the twang against my fingers when I hang clothes to dry. I make the line shiver, the strings on a fiddle. Shirts bow to pink petticoats. Clothes swing to my music. Britches throw a leg over like they're climbing a fence.

Two old maids done lost their style
If you want to get lucky, you got to smile

Mellie Ivy's slim and has nice wavy hair, brown but there's something peculiar about her that makes me think of a birch when it's peeling, all that white papery bark curling away from something thick inside, something that's not white or papery at all. She puts the rouge on thick. She's Leola's friend, stranded, too.

I'll clap for the guitar boys but soft as if I'm wearing gloves.

There's Leola's band, Grundy, Andrew, Jake, but no Leola. Probably waiting to bring her on like the queen of surprises. It's a new fellow going to sing. But the voice—

Leola

In a man's suit. In her dead brother's clothes. His boots that I blacked and blacked, kept ready for him to come back across the waters and take up the plow again. Leola's chance blown up like Arthur's last view. A land mine, jagged light, then sweet blue air, like the morning he took his first step, careful already around the mud hole where the hound dog slept. His shoes dancing on the stage.

It's all I can see.

Them black boots, big hump-toed grins stomping the boards. Him. Arthur. And everybody laughing. The whole hall laughing and Leola a grin bigger than the boots as she sings, the pants tight and slim around her legs, the shirt starched just so, her hair hid in a bowler.

Pa's fidgeting, laughing to go along with the crowd, his hand weeping in mine. At home it will harden against me.

Gone. I should be gone. Each song long as cancer.

My fool girl.

Singing and dancing and hallooping all over the stage like a stable boy. I crisped the eyelet, crisped her hair, sewed the edges of the rags to hold her curls.

Mellie Ivy pink as a chigger.

Pa about to explode, about to walk up to the stage and jerk Leola from it, knock down the hat, pull off the pants and starched shirt and her dead brother's boots and make her stand up there like that, make her understand what she is.

I pray that he's too old, my hand in his vise, my hand crushed and swelling.

What They Wore
Kyle Hemmings

On a block of shanty bars in Golden Gai, Shinjuku, Nakata hangs on her laundry line the garments of each of her three ex-boyfriends, as if washing the clothes over and over will bring them back, as if every designer shirt or pair of baggy jeans is the outer trapping of a lost self.

Each boyfriend has told her in one way or another that she was not altogether. I am, she told each one, it's just that the parts don't always work in sync.

The black hoodie and cuffed shorts belonged to a boy named Junichi. He collected photos of old movie stars and told her that with her slim figure and beautiful navel, she reminded him of a 90s Kate Moss. After rainbow sex, he told her that she rolled her eyes while straddling him and her face turned darker shades of night. He asked her if she ever thought of someone else when with him, maybe, like holding a phantom.

She said that with him she watched phantoms rise from the bed. She said that sometimes she felt floating over the top of Mount Fuji, taking in 36 views.

He became obsessed with wearing her.

One night, they were caught in the rain. She washed his hoodie and shorts, gave him the clothes of a old boyfriend. Warming himself by her heater, still wearing her robe, he asked her how many times would she drown for him; how many poisonous lizards would she chase out of her bed. How many glass jars would she fill with her-for-him. Just for him.

She said that she only loved him in pieces.

The sound of the rain tapered. Until there was nothing.

And he became a ghost.

She hung his outerwear on the line.

At times, she swore he spoke to her through the lips of strangers. Each stranger said he would return.

The half-sleeve blazer and cargo pants belonged to a boy who was too withdrawn to come out of corners, who was in love with the virtual girl who Nakata resembled. He loved telling her how his lack of ambition made his post-war uncles sigh. With him, she wore heels so high, he called her dangerous. She promised to sow herself to his skin so he would feel real.

He said his virtual girlfriend was expecting their first child.

At night, she invented the virtual girlfriend's voice, the thousand shades of love, the heroic attempt at love at sunrise.

Nakata thought: I could be the virtual girlfriend.

When Nakata tried making love with him, he turned into a ghost.

She kept his blazer and pants.

She had a dream about the moon having a false pregnancy.

For nights, she cried. Outside her window, the sky was a swirl of orange and blue and red longings.

The graffiti style T-shirt and Panda print shorts belonged to the boy with twitching muscles, the one who performed tricks for her on street corners, jumped from rooftops, shoplifted in Shinjuku. Imitating a shogun warrior or super robot, he made her clap until her hands were too heavy to own.

He confided in her that when older, he will be a giant.

Or he would be a criminal catching criminals. He would join a biker gang.

They made love in panic-proofed rooms under shifting skies. Their love was superficially intense, could be bottled and exported. Increasingly, she felt diluted.

But she could watch him for hours juggling colored balls as if one of her many lives as a magic girl. He brought her night flowers that glowed. She gave him smoking mirrors and vague answers to his questions. His most persistent one: *Have you been cheating on me?*

In so many words, she hinted that she only loved him for his tricks and jokes and scams. He told her that if she didn't say that she loved him for who or what he was, he would walk out of her apartment, naked. He would make her the conversation piece of laughing birds.

She dared him.

He was hit by a car.

He became a ghost.

At night, she dreams now of their clothes taking on a life of their own. She leaves the window open. The T-shirt and the shorts, the hoodie and the half-sleeve blazer, fly into her room. The clothes stand before her. She's wearing a satin nightgown and rubbing sleep from her eyes. The clothes address her as "Princess."

The graffiti styled Tee shirt says You didn't love me enough.

The half-sleeve blazer says You tried to own me, but I was always immaterial.

The black hoodie says that he's come to realize that fragmented love is better than no love at all.

All articles of clothing agree that they should all stay friends.

You can always wear us if you get caught in the rain, they say.

There is no love, one says, like a ghostly love.

We want to stay on your laundry line, forever, they say.

In the morning, she makes herself breakfast, feels strangely out of place in the apartment, she lives in. She vows that she will never get caught in the rain again, will never turn another boy into a ghost.

Sipping instant coffee, she looks out the window, checks the laundry line, the same clothes, hanging in the gentle breeze, winkle-free--as if brand new.

Rural Vulture Meals
R. Gerry Fabian

A huge flocks of starlings
circles around
my grandmother's wash line.

She shakes the line
to scare them away.

They continue to circle.

I am seven and it's my first time
on the farm without my parents.

The old lady puts her basket down,
goes into the house
and returns with a shotgun
loaded with rock salt.

The explosion causes me to fall down
as well as five starlings.

"Get up," she chides.
"I warned them, plus the vultures
gotta eat."

Juneteenth
Nancy Flynn

Plymouth, Pennsylvania 1977

One more ordinary Sunday,
                        daybreak
hushed as a luckless lake. No
Father's Day flapjacks. No
Emancipation commemoration,
sips of Big Red vanilla cream
soda spiked with orange and lemon.
Rather diapers in an old wives' vinegar—
soak to the brim of a galvanized tub.
A kitchen coal stove cooled because it's hot.
A baby, five days old, asleep.
      Mere transitory,
your back-porch perch, impersonating
free. This first speck of moment-to-spare
and you stare a familiar spine,
caress its papery rush, anticipate
line after line in this book you've borne
for years:
> *People ask the way to Cold Mountain.*
> *Cold Mountain? There is no road that goes*
>   *through.*

         Morning
glories that strangle your defeated
victory gardening attempts. The clothes
-line, infinity's pulley above your head.
                    Circadian
church bells, you begin to think
a conspiracy, how they measure
each quarter-hour, how much
naptime you've got left.

Grand Canyon Mile 27: Wash Cycles
Karla Linn Merrifield

It'll all come out in the wash
my mother said, so as not to worry
about life's distractions & dilemmas:
grass stains, hangnails, Kennedy's assassination
& daddy's stranger behaviors

What comes out in the wash in these parts
is sand & scree in spring runoff, spring rains
down, down from canyon rim to river bed,
breaking free boulders bigger than my childhood
ranch house to raise rapids in my dory's course
as sure as I raised Cain for both my parents

So I wash my gritty laundry in an eddy
along the shore in shadow of Tiger Wash
There's a roaring in my head, riffles they must be
from deep sources below my rocks of human years:
It's a memory just starting to come out

All Between the Lines
A Personal Essay
Jan Hill

In my refrigerator, a water pitcher sits on the top shelf in front of the light. It is durable and practical, made of pressed glass, a farmer's pitcher. Each time I open the refrigerator and see the light pouring through the ribbed glass, it captures and holds my gaze like a fine art piece. I probably waste a lot of BTUs standing there admiring the effect, but I enjoy this bit of accidental perfection in a life that, over the years, has fallen far short of perfection in most things.

Another place I sense perfection is at my clothesline. Built next to the woods in a grassy field, it is 30 feet long, with six lines strung between sturdy posts. As early in spring as I can get out there without snowshoes, I haul my laundry from the basement to this clothesline. Just the thought of being able to hang laundry will get me out of bed early on a summer morning. My goal is practical, to dry the clothes, but when I start pinning those bright colors to the sky, I always feel like I am making art—ephemeral art. Here this morning, gone by nightfall.

If I were picking grapes in an arbor, ducking beneath damp vines early in the morning, the world could not feel any more luscious than this. As I walk between the lines, wet clothes flap against my hair and arms, a towel clings to my shoulder, a pair of pants settles temporarily on my head. Sometimes I grab a shirt and press it to my face, taking a long sniff, loving that singular *clean* smell of cool, wet fibers with a little hint of the man who wore it still circling around it. I will repeat my sniffing when the clothes are dry and warm in the afternoon. Both are intoxicating.

I always start by pinning anything colorless or shapeless to the far lines, then I hang the things I want to see from the house. Once the basket is empty, I start fiddling with the lines, making little adjustments, full of excuses not to go back indoors. If a sheet threatens to brush the grass, I rehang it; if a dinner napkin has gotten pinned to a separate line from its mates, I shift things around so they can hang together. I choose different organizing principles on different days: I might arrange by color, shape, wearer, or function, depending on my mood. When I stand back to look, I think of prayer flags—and this makes my heart sing.

In Wallace Stevens' poem "Anecdote of the Jar," a round jar on a wilderness hill transforms and orders that wilderness, instantly takes "dominion" of the surrounding landscape—at least in the perception of a poetic speaker who first manipulates, then interprets, the scene. The wilderness doesn't know it has been organized, the jar doesn't know it serves as organizing principle, and neither jar or wilderness knows it is in Tennessee and being observed by this great thinker poet. Of course scholars argue all the way to the moon and back about the poem's meaning and artistic merit, variously insisting this is a poem about the relationship between art and the natural world, emptiness, form and function, ideas of order, runaway development, imperialism, the poetic process itself, and more.

I just like to imagine Stevens stopping on a hill to eat a sandwich and drink from a canning jar, maybe take a little walk, then turn back and notice how his jar, perched in the middle of all this *nature*, dramatically changes—even subdues—what minutes ago seemed like wildness. I like to walk around in the poem, slowly soak in its images, pretend I am picknicking with Stevens himself, and think about how objects like jars or clotheslines can change the natural world around them into a bit of stage scenery—our eye naturally goes to the object. But I don't try to unlock the poem's meaning beyond that, because its arrangement of images, obtuse as some are, feels like perfection. Let it be.

I am attracted, maybe even addicted, to small and mostly useless thrift store finds, shiny little things—what my daughter Tracy called "pretties." I always spend time arranging them all when something new comes home—I line up my cream pitchers in various groupings on the oak sideboard, stack and unstack small pottery bowls on a shelf, shuffle antique spoons around on a rack—working toward something I can't name. But in the end I get bored arranging trinkets, maybe because, unlike my laundry, they have no life beyond their prettiness. Laundry, constantly moving between closets, human bodies, washing machine, and clothesline, is almost alive.

The one thing I can't seem to arrange is my days. Fall to spring is manageable, since I must keep to a teaching schedule. In summer, though, I rise early, ready to write while it's still cool, but by 10 a.m. I have still not made my way to the computer. I have probably sorted mail, dumped crumbs out of the toaster, scrubbed last night's stir-fry off the stovetop, moved the birdfeeders, even dusted shelves and rearranged the pretties-- but not written anything new.

But I did hang the clothes today! And I stood longer than usual to enjoy the arrangement of color, form, and function, admiring the beet-dyed cotton pants and bright blue t-shirt I had gardened in; the red and yellow fish-print napkins, wine-stained from a late-night dinner with friends; the rows of bright ankle socks, yellow with yellow, purple with purple, green with green—my summer slippers.

My clothesline organizes the wilderness, no argument there. With its splash of shapes and colors whipping in the wind against the woods, fields, wildflowers and weed patches, I see the land in a new way, a backdrop for my laundry to dance around and tell stories all day.

I suppose I could try to mine the mystery of my clothesline's allure more thoroughly, maybe find out if there are other people out there who find moments under a clothesline perfectly sublime. But in the end I don't think I can find a good answer. When people ask me why I don't just use my dryer, I usually say I want to save money and conserve the earth's resources, and that's true. But I should say that hanging laundry is as satisfying as arranging words on a page, as practical as a pitcher of cool water on a hot day, as sensual as crawling into bed with a lover, and sometimes, as full of potential for thinking about life's odd little truths as placing a jar on a hill in Tennessee.

Sheets for Clouds
J.M. Cogdell

Stuffy, I can't breathe. The crush of bodies, and the heat from the small kitchen, it's all too much. I murmur the appropriate replies making my way to the back door. I slip out welcoming the quiet and the cool afternoon air. In the middle of the yard, against the fading light, I spot what looks like a leaning cross. The irony is not lost as smiling I reach out and brush off a piece of rust from the lone pole. Hard to believe this rusted piece of steel, with the help of its missing twin, once held the imagination of three little girls, and the weight of Mama's sheets. The wind ruffles the leaves at my feet and memories flood my mind as I look down the hill at the fence that now separates the neighbors.

***

"Have you girls finished your cereal?" Mama comes in the kitchen setting the empty clothesbasket by the door.

"Yes, Mama." I answer for the three of us, helping Susie down from her chair.

"Then ya'll can go on out and play. But, don't go to the street, stay in the back yards. I'll be checking."

"Yes, ma'am." Our response sounds like a chorus.

We scoot outside letting the screen door slap just as we hear her yell *don't slam the screen door*. It happens every day, the slamming, and the yelling. In our back yard, we can see to the end of the neighborhood, all the way to the last house. On laundry day, it's an amazing sight of billowing sheets flying through the air. I love laundry day.

The three of us stand at the top of the hill and run at top speed squealing through the middle of Mama's sheets. I run with Daisy and Susie following me to the next line of clouds. We are angels flying through the sky, the sheets our clouds. We look more like three fuzzy bunnies with our blond curls and yellow sundresses bounding across the grass, than we do angels. Mama says dressing us alike, makes life simple for her. I'll be glad when I can pick out my own clothes.

"Shh," I stop my finger at my lips and hush my sisters. I point up at Mrs. Tyler's clothesline. Small white squares hung next to the sheets. That can mean only one thing.

"What's wrong Jan?"

"We gotta be real quiet going across Miz Tyler's yard. Those are diapers."

Both girls nod; my sisters understand that I know things about the world. "What that means is she must've had her new baby. So we better not wake a sleeping baby."

We tiptoe through Mrs. Tyler's sheets and under the diapers as we make our way to the next yard. After all angels must watch after babies, puppies, and kittens, I explain as we go.

There's a lot of sheets at Vernon's house; he still wets the bed, but I pretend I don't know. The cowboy sheets are a dead giveaway. He outta get his mama to use plain white. I don't mention this to the sisters. They're not very good at keeping secrets.

***

The wind picks up, and with a shiver, I pull my mind back to the present. Daisy waves to me from the back door.

"What you doing out here?" She brings my sweater. "Nip in the air, fall's coming early."

"Yes, but it's nice. I needed some air."

A chuckle escapes when Daisy notices the rusty pole. "I loved playing in the sheets. But I hated doing laundry when I got older."

"Me too." I wrap my arm around her. We turn hearing the familiar slap of the screen door.

"It's time to go." Susie walks toward us pulling on her coat. "Everybody's ready."

Here, we are the three of us together again, this time dressed in black. Mother would be pleased to see us dressed alike, keeps things simple. I wonder do we still appear as blond angels standing in mother's back yard. Fences make good neighbors; I believe is how the saying goes, but I'm not so sure that's true. Maybe all they do is separate people. Now no sheets flap in the wind or kids run between houses chasing clouds. The fences are too high. I hear no laughter on the wind or see angels in the clouds.

Hand in hand, we leave the lone pole, the only remnant of years past, clotheslines, and sheets billowing in the wind. We walk toward the waiting car, to say our last goodbye.

Prayer Flags
Judith Sornberger

I see now why each line of wash
in a backyard makes me want to drop
down on my knees, that I am witnessing
the prayer of t-shirts, blue jeans, sheets
and underwear—the prayer flapping
below terra cotta rooftops in Siena
repeated in the same tongue right here
in Tioga County, Pennsylvania.

Don't tell me those women don't know
they are praying. Have you ever
watched even a busy woman hanging
out the holy ghosts of her family?
Seen her stand there afterwards,
her empty basket resting like a child
on her cocked hip, as she adored
the spirit of the wind tossing them
into the deep blue mind of heaven?

Even a grieving woman feels her feet
lift from the earth when the breeze
kicks up the ankles of her drying khakis,
feels her shoulders sprouting wings
as her blouse takes flight. I don't know
if she is grateful as she clips each
garment to her line, or if each one
bodies forth a precious worry.
Maybe her clothesline is one long wail.

But watch her hours later
when she goes to bring her wash in,
leaning into the warm scent of sun
woven with birdsong, closing her eyes
for just a second as she guesses
this must be how God smells,
pulling each piece into an embrace
of folding, settling it in her basket,
and giving the whole stack a final pat.

Scat
Ryan Swofford

Mama hung the laundry line at midnight
usually she'd be smoking a cigarette
and burning holes though our shirts
with scat stains on them

You boys
she told us one midnight
need to stay away from them raccoons
they're rabid
they're fierce
they'll rip you to shreds

Mama told us
puffing on a cigarette
hanging a scat-stained shirt
you boys need to stay small
don't you ever become men

Whiteout
J.R. Kangas

About all I remember
of those weeks of radiation
are the puffy white clouds
drifting by my bedroom window
and the scads of bleached shorts
on the backyard clothesline.

At the Clothesline
Carol Hamilton

We women join in constellation,
our archetypal memories stirred
by the wind's capture in puffed
backs of shirts, white and smelling
of soap. Clothespins peg me
to ancient rites boiling up
in my blood, magic potions
combined for love. From pre-war
days on a Kansas City hill
my mother-in-law whispers to me
down her wiped clean wires
and my mother bends to her basket
on a prairie farm, hating it.
My lines are draped with branches
of an overgrown elm. The suggestions
was made that the rough metal poles
might be removed. But I keep
the four wires and their pinions,
visit them with damp, fresh offerings
and they, like a clever medium at
a séance, arouse the sleeping.

Contributor's Notes / scissors and spackle / Laundry Lines

Allie Marini Batts is an MFA candidate at Antioch University of Los Angeles, meaning she can explain deconstructionism, but cannot perform simple math. Her work has been nominated for Best of the Net and the Pushcart Prize. Her chapbook, *You Might Curse Before You Bless* was published in 2013 by ELJ Publications. Find her on the web: **https://www.facebook.com/YouMightCurseBeforeYouBless**

Erica Bodwell is a poet from Concord, New Hampshire. She has recently had poems appear in *Emerge Literary Journal, Red River Review, The Smoking Poet, Crack the Spine* and other fine journals.

Brenton Booth resides in Sydney, Australia. Work of his has been published in a variety of small press journals, most recently *Clutching at Straws, Boyslut, Red Fez, Thunder Sandwich, Dead Snakes, Commonline Journal, Clockwise Cat, 3AM Magazine, Dogzplot, Pyrokinection,* and *Unlikely Stories.*

Raised in Albuquerque, New Mexico, **Elena Saavedra Buckley** is a seventeen-year-old poet currently finding her bearings in the publishing world. Aside from her own work, Elena spends time editing pieces for the national student literary magazine Polyphony H.S. and re-reading the same Stevens poems over and over. She is the author of the classical music blog Neo Antennae (**http://neoantennae.blogspot.com/**) and is in love with Saturn, especially through her telescope.

Born in the Appalachian foothills of southern Ohio, **Lacie Clark-Semenovich** now lives and writes in the greater Cleveland area with her husband. Her poetry can be found in *Barrelhouse, Zygote in My Coffee, MOBIUS, Kansas City Voices, Eunoia Review,* and other journals. She is the author of a chapbook, *Legacies* (Finishing Line Press, 2012).

Brittany Nicole Connolly is currently pursuing her MFA in creative writing at the University of Tampa, while still managing to live in the hills of Greeneville, Tennessee. She is 24 years old, an avid cat devotee, and a lover of all things creative, bizarre, and fabulist. She is the Artisan Review Editor at *Connotation Press: An Online Artifact*, and her work has appeared in issues of *Quarter After Eight, The Sheepshead Review, The Alarmist, The Gulf Stream: Poems of the Gulf Coast,* and *Paper Darts.*

E. H. Brogan lives in Newark, Delaware. She graduated from the University of Delaware with a B.A. in English. She has had poems appear in *Corvus, Downer Magazine, Caesura,* and others. She's also a staff member and blog runner for *Kenning Journal* (www.kenningjournal.com). Currently she works in Wilmington, Delaware, for the banking industry.

Michael Cocchiarale is the author of *Still Time* (Fomite, 2012), a collection of short and shorter stories. His short fiction has appeared in *Fiction Fix, Northville Review, REAL, Stickman Review,* and others.

AS A WRITER OF LITERARY FICTION, **J.M. COGDELL**'S SHORT STORIES ARE AVAILABLE IN VARIOUS PUBLICATIONS INCLUDING; THE ANTHOLOGIES ONce Upon A Time, and *Flash Fiction World Vol-1 & Vol 2, Squawk Back Magazine, What The Dickens Magazine, YAREAH Magazine,* and *Angie's Diary Online Writing Magazine.* She is a Yahoo Contributor and a member of the Writers' Guild of Texas. She currently lives in Texas. Read more on her blog at www.jeanswriting.com.

Emily Rose Cole is an emerging poet, folksinger, and MFA hopeful currently residing in Indianapolis. Her debut solo album, "I Wanna Know," was released in May of 2012. Her poetry has appeared in several publications, including *Amethyst Arsenic, Punchnel's, Third Wednesday, Short, Fast and Deadly,* and *Eunoia Review.*

R. Gerry Fabian is a retired English instructor and editor of *Raw Dog Press*. http://rawdogpress.bravesites.com/ He has published in various little and literary magazines since 1970. Currently, he is putting the finishing touches on a poetry manuscript of his published poetry and searching for a publisher.

Nancy Flynn hails from the coal country of northeastern Pennsylvania and spent many years living on a creek in Ithaca, New York. In 1998, she married the scientist whose house once hosted parties where Vladimir Nabokov chain-smoked cigarettes. They packed up their Conestoga Volvo 850 and headed for the foothills of the Oregon Coast Range, finally settling in Portland in 2007. More about her past lives and publications can be found at www.nancyflynn.com.

Jennifer Freed lives with her family in Central Mass, where she raises her daughters, writes, and tutors refugees in English and life-skills. Her poetry appears or is upcoming in *Poetry East*, *Theodate*; *The Worcester Review*; *The Christian Science Monitor*; *Cloudbank*, and others. It is anthologized in *The Cancer Poetry Project 2* and *Inner Landscapes: Writers Respond to the Art of Virginia Dehn*.

Dana Green received her MFA from the University of Massachusetts in Amherst and is currently a PhD candidate at the University of Denver. She lives by mountains with a husky and cat.

Andrei Guruianu is a Romanian-born writer currently living in New York City where he teaches in the Expository Writing Program at New York University. He is the author of a memoir, *Metal and Plum* (Mayapple Press, 2010) and four collections of poetry, most recently *Postmodern Dogma* (Sunbury Press, 2011). In the past he has served as editor and publisher of the literary journal *The Broome Review* and guest editor of the internationally distributed magazine *Yellow Medicine Review*. In 2009 and 2010 he served as Broome County, NY's first poet laureate. More at www.andreiguruianu.com

Carol Hamilton has recent publications in *South Carolina Review*, *Poet Lore*, *Tulane Review*, *slipstream*, *River Oak Review*, *Tar River Review*, *San Pedro River Review*, *Willow Review*, *White Wall Review*, *Bryant Literary Review* and others. She has been nominated five times for a Pushcart Prize. She has published 15 books of children's novels, legends and poetry, most recently, *Master Of Theater: Peter The Great* and *Lexicography*. She is a former Poet Laureate of Oklahoma.

William Ogden Haynes is a poet and author of short fiction from Alabama who was born in Michigan and grew up a military brat. His first book of poetry entitled *Points of Interest* appeared in 2012 and a second collection of poetry and short stories *Uncommon Pursuits* was published in 2013. Both are available on Amazon in Kindle and paperback. He has also published over seventy poems and short stories in literary journals and his work has been anthologized multiple times.

Kyle Hemmings is the author of several chapbooks of poems: *Avenue C*, *Cat People*, and *Anime Junkie* (Scars Publications). His latest ebook is *You Never Die in Wholes* from *Good Story Press*. His favorite band of all time is Love and he is a big fan of Roky Erickson. He lives and writes in New Jersey.

Jan Hill lives in Northfield, Minnesota, where she teaches writing, women's studies, journalism, and children's literature at St. Olaf College. She has worked as an editor, technical writer, and reporter, and published essays in *South Dakota Review*, *Moxie*, *Midday Moon* and *Meta4* as well as news stories, critical essays, children's literature author bios, and encyclopedia articles on the literature of the Spanish Civil War.

Brian Hobbs has found this year to be one of the best of his life. He has gotten published in a bunch of amazing publications such as *scissors and spackle*, *Crack the Spine*, *Yorick Magazine*, *Red Fez*, *Milk Sugar Literary Magazine* and *Broadkill Review*. He will write till his ideas no longer hold him up. His two favorite people are his wife and his one year old daughter. He keeps trying to get his daughter to like peas. Something must be wrong if she doesn't like peas. I mean, come on.

A.J. Huffman has published five solo chapbooks and one joint chapbook through various small presses. Her sixth solo chapbook will be published in October by Writing Knights Press. She is a Pushcart Prize nominee, and the winner of the 2012 Promise of Light Haiku Contest. Her poetry, fiction, and haiku have appeared in hundreds of national and international journals, including *Labletter*, *The James Dickey Review*, *Bone Orchard*, *EgoPHobia*, *Kritya*, and *Offerta Speciale*, in which her work appeared in both English and Italian translation. She is also the founding editor of Kind of a Hurricane Press. www.kindofahurricanepress.com

Rosemary Jones is an Australian living and teaching in the U.S. Her fiction has appeared in magazines that include *Denver Quarterly*, *Sonora Review*, *Gargoyle*, *Spinoza Blue*, *Corium Magazine*, and has been read on Australian national radio. Her nonfiction has recently appeared in Creative Nonfiction and Brain, Child.

J.R. Kangas works as an academic librarian and as a musician, and have had work in many magazines including *Atlanta Review*, *Connecticut Review*, *The New York Quarterly*, and *West Branch*.

Philip Kobylarz lives in the East Bay of San Francisco. Recent work of his appears or will appear in *Tampa Review*, *Apt*, *Santa Fe Literary Review*, *New American Writing*, *Prairie Schooner*, *Poetry Salzburg Review* and has appeared in *Best American Poetry*. His book, *rues*, has recently been published by Blue Light Press of San Francisco, his short story collection and essay/memoire/philosophical travelogue are forthcoming.

Lisa Fusch Krause lives in Seattle, Washington, with her husband and two black cats. As a long-time professional editor, she is immersed in words for a living. Lisa has published both poetry and prose in places such as CAHOODALOODALING, CASCADIA REVIEW, THE FAR FIELD, and RESPUESTAS: THE NERUDA PROJECT as well as previously in SCISSORS AND SPACKLE. She thinks of her writing in terms of "snapshots," capturing images and moments of time.

Sarah Kravitz is a California native, writer, and former high school teacher with an English degree from UC Berkeley. Currently, she is pursuing a doctorate in psychology. Her work has been published or is forthcoming in *Bop Dead City*, *Stone Highway Review*, *The Citron Review* and other journals.

Gabrielle Lee is an MFA candidate at Eastern Washington University, where she works as an assistant managing editor for *Willow Springs*. She lives in Spokane, Washington with her husband but misses her native California dearly. Originally from Fresno, she lived in southern California for five years, where she earned her BFA in Dance Choreography and BA in English from the University of California, Irvine and mastered the art of sitting in traffic. She has recently written a short play that will be performed as part of the Spokane Playwrights' Festival in mid-May.

C. Beth Loofe

Tom Luddecke lives in the center of Connecticut, just far enough from Boston and New York City to be considered insignificant. He is recently retired from his real job, leaving him more time now to make up things. At this stage in his life, he feels he has nothing left to disprove His humorous pieces have appeared in such places as *The Rusty Nail*, *Humor Press*, *Postcard Shorts*, *the Short Humor Site*, *The Hartford Courant*, and his family's nightmares.

Richard Luftig is a professor of educational psychology and special education at Miami University in Ohio now residing in Pomona, CA. He is a recipient of the Cincinnati Post-Corbett Foundation Award for Literature and a semi finalist for the Emily Dickinson Society Award. His poems have appeared in numerous literary journals in the United States and
internationally in Japan, Canada, Australia, Europe, Thailand, Hong Kong and India. One of his published poems was nominated for the 2012 Pushcart Poetry Prize.

Katherine MacCue is a Pushcart Prize-nominated poet who lives in New York. She graduated from the George Washington University where she studied the French language and History. She has been published in various journals including *decomP magazinE* and *Stone Highway Review*. She enjoys rainy days along the shore and spending time with her family. You can reach her at her blog thenearlyfamous.blogspot.com.or via email at kmacc@gwu.edu."

Award-winning poet and National Park Artist-in-Residence, **Karla Linn Merrifield** has had nearly 300 poems appear in dozens of journals and anthologies. She has seven books to her credit, the newest of which is *The Ice Decides: Poems of Antarctica* (Finishing Line Press). Forthcoming from Salmon Poetry is *Athabaskan Fractal and Other Poems of the Far North*, Her *Godwit: Poems of Canada*. (FootHills) received the 2009 Eiseman Award for Poetry. She is assistant editor and poetry book reviewer for *The Centrifugal Eye* (www.centrifugaleye.com). Visit her blog, Vagabond Poet, at http://karlalinn.blogspot.com.

Amanda Hart Miller is presently pursuing a Master of Arts in Writing at Johns Hopkins University, and she teaches creative writing and literature classes at a community college in Maryland. Her work has appeared in *PANK*, *Literary Mama*, *Apeiron Review* and elsewhere, and her early reader chapter book entitled *SuperDylan and the Powers of Just Right* will debut this summer. She blogs at amandahartmiller.com.

Jason Lee Miller, MFA, is a curriculum developer and composition instructor at Eastern Kentucky University. His work --poetry, fiction, essays, and book reviews--have appeared in *94 Creations*, *Blood Lotus*, *Bluegrass Accolade*, *Copperfield Review*, *Danse Macabre Du Jour*, *Dew on the Kudzu*, *Gloom Cupboard*, *The Legendary*, *Milk Sugar*, *Numinous*, *Ontologica*, *State of Imagination*, and *Subliminal Interiors*. Sporadically, he updates a blog: Offtopic.typepad.com.

Mirabella Mitchell is a graduating senior at Princeton University and in the fall will join the University of Virginia MFA program. Her work is forthcoming in *Emerge Literary Journal*.

Linda Niehoff's stories have appeared or are forthcoming in *Crack the Spine*: Spring 2013 Anthology, *Literary Orphans*, *Forge* and *Circa Review*. She has been a finalist in *Glimmer Train*'s Very Short Fiction Award and Short Story Award for New Writers.

Deonte Osayande is a poet and youth activist from Detroit, Mi. He's currently a Masters student at the University of Detroit Mercy and teaches poetry and creative writing in high schools for Inside Out Detroit. His work can be found in *Emerge Literary Journal*, *Wayne Literary Review*, *Eunoia Review*, and many publications.

Genevieve Payne was born and raised in Maine. She now splits her time between Maine and Central New York.

Lynn Pruett teaches in the low-residency MFA program at Murray State University. She's published one novel, *Ruby River* (Atlantic Monthly Press) published and stories most recently in the *Michigan Quarterly Review*, *Border Crossing*, the *Louisville Review*, and elsewhere.

henry 7. reneau, jr. writes words in fire to wake the world ablaze & illuminated by courage that empathizes with all the awful moments: a freight train bearing down with warning that blazes from the heart, like a chambered bullet exploding inadvertently.

April Salzano teaches college writing in Pennsylvania and is working on her first several collections of poetry and an autobiographical novel on raising a child with Autism. Her work has appeared in *Poetry Salzburg*, *Convergence*, *Ascent Aspirations*, *The Rainbow Rose*, *The Camel Saloon*, *The Applicant*, *The Mindful Word*, *The Weekenders Magazine*, *Deadsnakes*, *Montucky Review*, *Daily Love*, *Visceral Uterus*, *Crisis Chronicles*, *Windmills*, and is forthcoming in *Inclement*, *Poetry Quarterly*, *Decompression*, *Work to a Calm*, *Bluestem*, and *Connotation Press*. April also serves as co-editor for several online journals at *Kind of a Hurricane Press*.

Mary Lee Sauder is an undergraduate Creative Writing and Interactive Media Studies double major at Miami University in Ohio. She is from the very small town of Archbold, Ohio, where there are more cornstalks than people.

Eileen Ni Shuilleabhain grew up in the gaelic speaking region of Connemara on the west coast of Ireland. She now lives and works in Galway city as a Social worker and Psychotherapist. Her work was previously published in *Aperçus Quarterly*, *Boyne Berries*, *Emerge Literary Journal* and *The Galway Review*.

M. E. Silverman is editor of *Blue Lyra Review*. He moved from New Orleans to Georgia and teaches at Gordon State College. His chapbook, *The Breath before Birds Fly* (ELJ Publications, 2013), is available. His poems have appeared in over 70 journals, including: *Crab Orchard Review*, *32 Poems*, *Chicago Quarterly Review*, *Tapestry*, *The Southern Poetry Anthology*, *The Los Angeles Review*, *Mizmor L'David Anthology: The Shoah*, *Cloudbank*, *Neon*, *Many Mountains Moving*, *Pacific Review*, *Because I Said So Anthology*, *Sugar House Review*, and other magazines. M. E. Silverman was a finalist for the 2008 New Letters Poetry Award, the 2008 DeNovo Contest and the 2009 *Naugatuck River Review* Contest. He is working on editing a contemporary Jewish anthology with Deborah Ager forthcoming in 2013 from Bloomsbury.

Catherine Simpson is a cellist who lives in Santa Barbara. She has been previously published in the *Big River Poetry Review*, *Right Hand Pointing*, *Spectrum*, *Step Away Magazine*, and *Into the Teeth of the Wind*.

Carol Smallwood co-edited Women on Poetry: Writing, Revising, Publishing and Teaching (McFarland, 2012) on the list of Best Books for Writers by Poets & Writers Magazine; Women Writing on Family: Tips on Writing, Teaching and Publishing (Key Publishing House, 2012); Compartments: Poems on Nature, Femininity, and Other Realms (Anaphora Literary Press, 2011) received a Pushcart nomination. Carol has founded, supports humane societies. Excerpt from Lily's Odyssey, a novel, published with permission by *All Things That Matter Press*; its first chapter's a Short List Finalist for the Eric Hoffer Award for Best New Writing http://www.pw.org/content/carol_smallwood

Michael J. Soloway grew up eating oranges, catching lizards, and listening to the gasp of tennis ball cans being opened in south Florida. He received his Masters Degree in Creative Writing from Wilkes University and will earn his MFA in November. In addition, Michael has served as managing editor of more than a dozen nonprofit magazines and just finished his first memoir *Share the Chameleon*, about attempting to break his family's cycle of abuse, as he becomes a father for the first time in his 40s. *Brevity Magazine* published Michael's short essay, "Introducing Mother Nature," in 2012. In addition, *Split Lip* magazine published his nonfiction essay, "Sticks and Stones," about his grandmother's slide into dementia, in March 2013. His work has also appeared in *Red Fez*, *Pithead Chapel*, *Serving House: A Journal of Literary Arts*, and *Under the Gum Tree* magazines. An excerpt from *Share the Chameleon* will appear in *Split Lip* magazine in September. Michael was recently named managing editor of *Split Lip* and "Stick and Stones" has been nominated for Sundress Publication's *Best of the Net Anthology*. Also an accomplished playwright, Michael's first 10-minute play, "I Love You Lynn Swann," was produced by the Pittsburgh New Works Festival this fall.

Judith Sornberger's latest poetry collection WAL-MART ORCHID won Evening Street Press's Helen Kay Chapbook Prize. Her full-length poetry book OPEN HEART is from Calyx Books. She has four other poetry chapbooks. After "graduating" from her career in university teaching, she now write full-time from her home on the side of a mountain outside Wellsboro, PA.

RL Swihart currently lives in Long Beach, CA, and teaches high school mathematics in Los Angeles. His poems have appeared in various online and print journals, including *Bateau, elimae, Rhino, Right Hand Pointing, 1110,* and *decomP*. His first collection of poems, *The Last Man*, was published in 2012 by *Desperanto Press*.

Ryan Swofford is a young writer living in the Pacific Northwest. He edits his own e-zine, called *The Weekenders* (theweekendersmagazine.blogspot.com). You can also find him on Facebook.

Diana Rae Valenzuela only wears black boots because all of her other shoes fell apart at the exact same time (that's why). She still has a tattoo of an "X" on her left thumb from a short-lived straight-edge period. She is twenty-one, ten months, and two days. Once, a rock fell out of her ear. She writes.

Changming Yuan, 4-time Pushcart nominee and author of *Allen Qing Yuan*, holds a PhD in English, tutors, and edits *Poetry Pacific* in Vancouver (Poetry submissions welcome at **yuans@shaw.ca**). Yuan's poetry appears in 689 literary publications across 26 countries, including *Asian Literary Review, Barrow Street, Best Canadian Poetry (2009, 2012), BestNewPoemsOnline, LiNQ, London Magazine* and *Threepenny Review*.